C000177757

GREAT
BRITISH
CHEFS

First published in Great Britain in 2021 by Food Publishing (Books) Limited
Great British Chefs
greatbritishchefs.com

ISBN 978-1-913933-08-1

Lead Recipe Developer & Food Stylist: Pollyanna Coupland
Photographer: Sim Canetty-Clarke
Project Lead: Mark Gandy
Editor: Tom Shingler
Assistant Home Economists: Henry Coldstream and Alex Dodson
Design: NO Branding Limited

Printed and bound by TEAM in Leeds, UK

Thank you to all the wonderful chefs who have
shared their recipes with us for this book,
along with our fantastic partners:

Le Creuset / lecreuset.co.uk
Aubrey Allen / aubreyallen.co.uk
The Fish Society / thefishsociety.co.uk
Sofia Ceramics / sofiaceramics.com

Contents

Welcome

The process of taking a collection of raw ingredients and transforming them into a dish greater than the sum of its parts is – for those of us that love cooking – one of the most enjoyable ways to spend our time. It can be something as simple as dressing a salad, teasing out the natural flavours of the leaves and finding that perfect balance of flavour with salt, oil, acidity and sweetness, or something as complex as a slow-cooked ragù, waiting patiently for all the aromas to meld together in sumptuous harmony. And while the act of cooking may be something many of us tackle on our own, being able to share our creations with others is just as (if not more) rewarding.

So many of our social lives revolve around food because it's something that brings everyone together. Dinner parties at the dining table; barbecues in the fleeting British summertime; a few informal snacks or quick bites while catching up with friends – even the daily ritual of being called down when dinner's ready as a child. All these moments give us a chance to take a break from our lives and simply interact with one another. The food isn't always the most important part of these experiences, but it certainly doesn't hurt if what's put down in front of you is as good as the company.

This cookbook was put together during the coronavirus lockdowns the world faced throughout 2020 and 2021 – a time when chances to enjoy a meal with those we didn't live with were fleeting. It made many of us realise how much we missed occasions we previously took for granted, particularly inviting friends and family over for dinner. As society started to open up again, hosting and entertaining was what we wanted to do the most – first in our gardens, then, as restrictions relaxed, inside our homes. That desire to cook for others after being unable to for so long was what inspired every single one of the fantastic recipes inside this book.

With seven chapters encompassing dishes suited to every social occasion, there's something for everyone and recipes suited to home cooks of all skill levels. There are small, tapas-style plates designed to be mixed and matched for casual get-togethers with friends; bountiful platters and hearty one pots to bring to the table so everybody can help themselves; light bites, nibbles and barbecue-friendly fare for entertaining in the garden and a selection of impressive starters, mains and desserts for more traditional dinner parties (with plenty of make-ahead elements so you don't have to spend hours in the kitchen away from your guests).

The first seven recipes in each chapter come from Great British Chefs' own Pollyanna Coupland, who has spent years developing dishes full of cheffy twists but with the home cook in mind. They're then followed by three recipes from some of the most exciting chefs cooking in the UK today, giving you a chance to bring a little bit of restaurant magic into your own kitchen. The chefs featured in this book are an eclectic bunch; a mix of emerging talent and time-honoured culinary masters. What brings them all together is their love of cooking for those that visit their restaurants – that same feeling home cooks get when they've spent that little bit of extra time and effort to create something special, just to put a smile on someone else's face.

We hope you enjoy cooking from this book as much as we enjoyed putting it together. Most of all, however, we hope that it gives you the inspiration needed to create dishes which provide a backdrop to seeing and entertaining friends and family. Our fondest memories are formed in all sorts of settings and situations, but for many of us – if you really think about it – the ones we cherish the most are formed over a meal with those we love whilst chatting, laughing and being around the table.

Al Fresco

One Pots

Make-Ahead Desserts

Adam Bennett p88
The Cross at Kenilworth, Warwickshire

As chef director of Michelin-starred 'restropub' The Cross at Kenilworth since 2013, Adam has been immersed in the world of fine dining since his teenage years. Using his decades of experience to create relaxed, accessible, lauded food, Adam's dishes are always expertly cooked, perfectly balanced and champion the natural flavours of the fantastic ingredients he uses above all else.

Angel Zapata Martin p36
Barrafina and Parrillan, London

Few chefs cooking in the UK today understand the flavours of Catalonia – and Spain in general – quite like Angel. As executive chef across London's celebrated Barrafina tapas restaurants (one of which holds a Michelin star) along with his grill-it-yourself outdoor restaurant Parrillan, any dish he turns his hand to instantly transports the diner to sunnier Spanish climes.

Ben Tish p63
Norma, London

Chef, restaurateur and cookbook author Ben Tish has a stellar track record for creating dishes that, quite simply, everyone wants to eat. With a love for all things Mediterranean and in particular the North-African-meets-Italian flavours of the island of Sicily, his acclaimed restaurant Norma offers one of those rare menus where it's almost impossible to choose what to taste first.

Charlie Hibbert p107
Ox Barn at Thyme, Cotswolds

After learning the ins and outs of cooking from
none other than Quo Vadis' Jeremy Lee, Charlie
returned home to his family's ambitious 'village
within a village' country retreat Thyme to head up
the kitchen at Ox Barn. Armed with a cornucopia of
homegrown produce from the surrounding fields, his
accomplished dishes are always honest, comforting
and cooked with love.

Graham Hornigold p178
Pastry consultant and owner of Longboys, London

If restaurateurs want their dessert menus to be the
best around, Graham is the man they turn to. After
working in some of the capital's finest hotels he
launched his own pastry consultancy business Smart
Patisserie, which sees him travel the world to help
develop inimitable desserts. Meanwhile, his London-
based Longboys shops offer the best doughnuts
you'll ever eat.

Harriet Mansell p60
Robin Wylde, Lyme Regis

Harriet began cooking professionally after finishing a
university degree and soon found herself working on
superyachts for high-profile clients as a private chef.
When she decided to return to land she set up shop
in Lyme Regis to open her own restaurant Robin
Wylde, where seasonal, locally grown and foraged
ingredients make up a beautiful, natural menu that
perfectly encapsulates the Dorset coastline.

Kerth Gumbs p130, p157

When representatives from Le Cordon Bleu cookery school travelled to Anguilla, the tiny Caribbean island where Kerth grew up, he knew he had to move to London and learn to cook. Most recently the executive chef at Ormer Mayfair, Kerth's playful yet classically rooted cooking style made him – and his food – an instant hit, effortlessly combining British ingredients with international flavours.

Luke French p35
Jöro, Sheffield

One of the most exciting chefs to emerge in recent years, Luke's modern, daring dishes pack as much flavour as humanly possible into every bite. With a particular love for Asian cuisines, he uses far-flung concepts, techniques and ingredients to elevate British produce like few others. A meal at his flagship restaurant Jöro in Sheffield is always full of intrigue and innovation.

Mark Dodson p133, p159
The Masons Arms, Devon

Mark opened The Masons Arms – a sleepy pub in the middle of the Devonshire countryside – in 2005 after decades of experience in top kitchens (including the Roux family's legendary restaurant The Waterside Inn). His food combines classical French techniques with local British ingredients to create Michelin-starred dishes that only a true master of the craft could accomplish.

Masaki Sugisaki p32
Dinings SW3, London

A traditionally trained Japanese chef, Masaki's creative flair meant moving away from the strict culinary rules of his home country to create a fusion-led approach to modern Japanese food in London. At Dinings SW3, his ability to impart Japanese techniques and flavours onto western dishes has won him legions of fans. The way he presents and plates food is unmatched in its beauty.

Matt Beardmore p87
Legare, London

The rustic, seasonal Italian dishes executive chef Matt Beardmore cooks in the kitchen of Legare are punchy, packed with flavour and a testament to just how incredible Italy's regional cuisine can be. His unfussy approach to creating the traditional dishes of the country – with the odd British influence thrown in – results in some of the most enjoyable Italian food in the capital.

Roberta Hall-McCarron p181
The Little Chartroom, Edinburgh

Edinburgh's own Roberta shines a spotlight on Scottish produce at her restaurant The Little Chartroom – a homely, welcoming place that serves a concise menu of familiar dishes with interesting twists. Inspired by the country's coastline, her experience in Michelin-starred kitchens ensures every exquisite plate sent out from the pass is cooked to perfection.

Rohit Ghai p111
Kutir, London

Rohit was the man responsible for some of London's most beloved Michelin-starred Indian restaurants before he set out on his own to open Kutir in a quaint Chelsea townhouse. Serving modern, innovative takes on dishes from India's varied regions, his knowledge of the country's cuisine, mastery of spicing and ability to take traditional flavours and reimagine them is unparalleled.

Sam Buckley p83
Where The Light Gets In, Stockport

Sustainability is a key part of the menu at Sam's destination restaurant – but not at the expense of terrific flavours and inventive dishes. By sourcing produce from his own farm, preserving what's in season for later in the year and working with by-products to minimise waste, he creates regularly changing menus which offer clever new ways of cooking and enjoying food.

Santiago Lastra p59
KOL, London

'Mexican soul, British ingredients' is the tagline for Santiago's smash-hit restaurant KOL, neatly summing up his unique approach to cooking in just four words. By working with the seasons and incorporating the UK's produce into bold, bright and incredibly flavoured Mexican dishes, he creates menus that are both a joy to eat your way through and can't be found anywhere else in the world.

Shaun Hill p129, p154
The Walnut Tree, Abergavenny

A true legend of the British food scene, Shaun has spent over half a century delighting diners with his unpretentious yet inspirationally delicious food. Soaking up all the knowledge he can from cookbooks and his travels around the globe, his classical-yet-contemporary dishes may look simple on the plate – but there's a wealth of technical expertise behind every element.

Stosie Madi p108
Parkers Arms, Lancashire

A whirlwind of talent and skill in the kitchen (which she runs almost single-handedly), Stosie has made rural inn the Parkers Arms one of the most beloved gastropubs in the country. Taking the best of local produce and adding a sprinkle of exciting international flavours into her recipes, her unbridled passion for all things culinary shines through in everything she cooks.

Stuart Collins p182
Docket No.33, Shropshire

After working with the likes of Gary Rhodes, Michael Caines and Gordon Ramsay, Stuart Collins set out on his own to open Docket No. 33, a small but perfectly formed restaurant in the market town of Whitchurch in Shropshire. His years of experience working at the very top combined with a love of using local ingredients results in truly memorable food in relaxed, welcoming surroundings.

Cook's Notes

As always, the better quality your ingredients, the better your dishes will taste. We always recommend using free-range produce wherever possible, as well as seeking out top-quality meat, fish and vegetables from butchers, fishmongers, greengrocers, farm shops and markets. Using good produce is a guaranteed way to massively increase the quality of your cooking – we used fish from The Fish Society and meat from Aubrey Allen for this book, which we can thoroughly recommend.

If you are using a fan-assisted oven, reduce the temperature to 20°C lower than the recipe states. However, keep in mind that all ovens vary slightly.

All teaspoon and tablespoon measurements are level.

Eggs should always be free-range and large in size (unless otherwise stated).

Onions, shallots and garlic should always be peeled before being used (unless otherwise stated).

Instructions for seasoning can be found in all the recipes, but always taste as you cook and tweak the amounts depending on personal preference. If the amount of salt or pepper is measured then it is included in the ingredients, but if it is just used to season a dish to taste then it won't be. We've never encountered a home cook who doesn't have salt and pepper in their kitchen, so we're assuming you'll always have them to hand!

Always read a recipe in full before tackling it at home to avoid any surprises along the way. Certain elements can usually be prepared or made in advance which makes serving much easier, so plan ahead and ensure you have everything you need.

Finally, we all have days where we want a true professional to cook and serve us food. The hospitality industry has been hit hard since the coronavirus pandemic, so we eagerly encourage you to get out and eat at the restaurants of the chefs included in this book if you are able to.

Small Plates

Battered cod cheeks with pea ketchup

Battered fish is a national treasure, and this recipe replaces the usual fillets with cod cheeks – a meatier, underused part of the fish that has a natural nugget shape just begging for some batter. On the side, the pea and malt vinegar ketchup provides a fresh, tart dip to cut through the richness. Enjoy with a glass of white wine or beer; a side dish of chips or fried potatoes is optional but thoroughly recommended.

Makes around 20
Cooking time: 1 hour
Equipment: Blender

Cod cheeks

160g of self-raising flour, plus extra for dusting

40g of cornflour

230ml of lager, chilled

500g of cod cheeks, trimmed of any sinew

Vegetable oil, for deep-frying

Malt vinegar, to season

Pea ketchup

½ shallot, roughly chopped

1 garlic clove, roughly chopped

300g of frozen peas, defrosted

3 sprigs of basil, or wild garlic if in season

25ml of malt vinegar

50ml of water

50ml of vegetable oil, plus extra for frying

Begin by making a batter. Whisk together both flours with the lager and a pinch of salt until the mixture has the consistency of double cream. Leave to rest in the fridge.

To make the ketchup, add a dash of oil to a small saucepan and gently cook the shallot and garlic for 5 minutes until soft and translucent. Leave to cool, then transfer to a blender with the peas, basil (or wild garlic), vinegar and water. Blitz until smooth, then with the motor still running, pour in the vegetable oil in a thin stream until the mixture emulsifies slightly (you may not need to use all the oil).

Pass the ketchup through a fine sieve for an extra smooth finish, then season to taste with salt and store in the fridge until needed. This ketchup can be made in advance but it will lose its vivid colour after 24 hours, so it's best to make it fresh.

Place a deep, heavy pan of oil over a high heat and wait until it reaches 180°C.

Ensure there is no remaining sinew on the cod cheeks, then pat them dry. If they are particularly large, then you can cut them into nugget-sized chunks – you want around 20 pieces in total. Take the batter out of the fridge and give it a little whisk to ensure it's well combined. Working in batches, dust each cod cheek in a little flour, dip it into the batter then add it straight to the hot oil. Deep-fry for around 4-5 minutes, until golden and crisp – you may need to flip the cheeks over halfway through cooking depending on how deep the pan is.

Drain the cod cheeks on kitchen paper, season with salt and a splash of malt vinegar, then serve with a bowl of the pea ketchup on the side.

Polenta-crusted halloumi with preserved lemon sauce

Few things are as tempting as freshly fried halloumi served hot from the pan. Here, the cheese is given extra crunch thanks to a polenta and coriander crust, with a sweet-meets-salty four-ingredient sauce brimming with the citrussy flavour of preserved lemons for drizzling and dipping. Any leftover sauce is particularly good for dipping falafel into or serving with lamb koftas.

Serves 2-4
Cooking time: 25 minutes

Halloumi

1 tsp coriander seeds

50g of polenta

½ tsp chilli powder (optional)

1 block (225g) of halloumi

1 egg, beaten with a pinch of salt

1 tbsp vegetable oil

Preserved lemon sauce

100g of preserved lemons, drained

100g of caster sugar

1 tsp honey

½ tsp black peppercorns, crushed

Begin by making the sauce. Cut the preserved lemons into quarters and remove any seeds, then finely chop. Place in a small pan over a medium heat with the sugar, honey and crushed peppercorns. Bring to a simmer then cook for around 5 minutes, stirring regularly, until you achieve a loose dropping consistency (a lot like sweet chilli sauce). Leave to cool slightly.

Toast the coriander seeds in a hot dry pan for 30 seconds then transfer to a pestle and mortar and crush. Mix the crushed seeds with the polenta and chilli powder, then scatter the mixture onto a small tray.

Cut the halloumi into 1cm slices and place the beaten egg in a bowl. Dip the halloumi slices into the egg then dab each side in the polenta mix. They don't need to be completely covered, so just focus on the widest sides.

Place a non-stick frying pan over a high heat and add the vegetable oil. Once hot, carefully add the crusted halloumi and fry for a few minutes on each side until the crust is golden and the halloumi inside is soft and beginning to melt. Serve immediately with the lemon sauce either drizzled over the cheese or on the side for dipping.

Wild garlic malfatti

Malfatti (meaning 'misshapen') are a sort of gnocchi-dumpling hybrid from Tuscany in Italy and are immensely comforting to eat. We've included wild garlic leaves – a harbinger of British springtime – to give them a little twist, but if wild garlic is out of season you can just use more spinach instead. Both the malfatti and the sauce can be made a day in advance if desired.

Serves 6
Cooking time: 1 hour
plus 1 hour straining time and cooling time

Malfatti

250g of ricotta

450g of spinach

50g of wild garlic leaves, with any flowers reserved for garnish

1 egg

50g of plain flour

50g of semolina, plus extra for dusting

70g of Parmesan, finely grated

1 pinch of nutmeg

1 lemon, zested

Tomato sauce

2 tins (800g) of chopped tomatoes

1 onion, peeled and halved through the root (so the layers stay together)

50g of unsalted butter

Begin by straining the ricotta. Line a sieve with a piece of muslin cloth (or j-cloth) and set over a bowl. Add the ricotta and leave to drain for around 1 hour in the fridge.

Meanwhile, make the sauce. Place the peeled onion halves in a pan with the tomatoes, a pinch of salt and the butter. Bring to a very low simmer, cook for 25 minutes then remove and discard the onion halves. Taste and season with salt and pepper; you can use a hand blender to blend into a smooth sauce or keep it chunky. Reserve in the fridge to reheat later.

To make the malfatti, wilt the spinach and wild garlic down with a pinch of salt in a wide pan. Transfer to a sieve and allow to cool, then squeeze out as much water as you can from the leaves. Finely chop, then place in a mixing bowl with the rest of the ingredients (including the strained ricotta). Season with a pinch of salt and pepper, then mix well until everything is evenly incorporated.

Roll the mixture into neat 2cm balls using your hands, then place on a tray dusted with semolina and leave in the fridge uncovered to firm up for at least 30 minutes (or overnight).

When ready to serve, bring a large pan of salted water to the boil and gently reheat the tomato sauce. Drop the malfatti into the water and cook for around 3 minutes, or until they float to the surface. Once cooked, drain and leave to steam-dry a little. At this point they are ready to eat, but you can also pan-fry them in a little butter or oil for a few minutes until lightly crisp.

Divide the sauce between serving plates. Place the malfatti on top and finish with a crack of black pepper and wild garlic flowers (if using).

Crispy merguez-stuffed olives with chilli honey

Deep-fried olives painstakingly stuffed with ragù are a speciality of Le Marche in Italy, where they're known as olives all'ascolana. Here, things are made a little easier by replacing the sauce with sausage, giving you something firmer to work with. It's a little bit fiddly but the results are incredible, offering up the perfect cluster of crunchy, briny, sweet orbs to be demolished in seconds. You could replace the sausage with slivers of mozzarella to make the dish vegetarian.

Serves 4
Cooking time: 45 minutes

Olives

170g of large pitted green olives, such as Gordal, drained

50g of merguez sausage, soft chorizo or a high-quality herbed sausage

25g of plain flour

1 large egg, beaten with a pinch of salt and a dash of milk

50g of panko breadcrumbs

Vegetable oil, for deep frying

Chilli honey

1 jar of honey

8 dried chillies

Begin by infusing the honey – you will have lots leftover but it can be used in all manner of dishes and will keep indefinitely. Roughly chop the chillies then add them to a hot dry pan and toast for a minute or so, until just starting to colour a little (but don't let them burn). Turn the heat right down then add the honey to the pan – you just want to warm the honey through so the chilli flavour infuses. Pour the honey and chillies back into the jar, then seal and set aside.

Pat the olives dry with kitchen paper. Split the sausage and remove the skin. Using your fingertips, pinch off little pea-sized pieces of the sausage meat and use the back of a teaspoon to poke and stuff them into the centre of the olives.

Set up a breadcrumbing station; a small bowl of flour, followed by a bowl with the beaten egg, a tray of the breadcrumbs and a clean plate to place the finished olives on. Dip the olives in the flour, then the egg and finally the breadcrumbs. Because of their slippery nature, the coating may slip off a bit – if this happens, dip them in egg and the breadcrumbs once again, using your hands to gently squeeze the crumbs onto the finished olive.

Bring a small pan of oil up to 180°C or until a breadcrumb added to the oil instantly sizzles and quickly turns golden. Once up to temperature, carefully lower the olives into the oil and deep-fry for 2-3 minutes, until golden and crisp. Work in batches if you need to. Drain on kitchen paper, place into small serving bowls and drizzle with a little chilli honey.

Haggis, neeps and tatties croquettes with whisky ketchup

Scotland's famous Burns Night dinner in a single bite with a whisky-infused dipping sauce on the side. Don't worry if you have haggis-haters in the vicinity; the flavour is far more mellow than the traditional dish. You can prepare the croquette filling a day in advance, too – just make sure you leave enough time for it to thaw slightly so you can slice it into croquettes before breadcrumbing.

Makes 20 croquettes
Cooking time: 2 hours 45 minutes
Equipment: Blender

Croquettes

500g of Maris Piper potatoes

20g of unsalted butter

50g of whole milk

150g of swede, peeled and finely diced

180g of cooked haggis, or vegetarian haggis, crumbled

1 dash of Worcestershire sauce

50g of plain flour

3 eggs, beaten with a dash of milk and a pinch of salt

150g of fine panko breadcrumbs

Vegetable oil, for deep-frying

Whisky ketchup

1 tbsp vegetable oil

½ onion, diced

2 garlic cloves, sliced

400g of ripe tomatoes, chopped

25ml of red wine vinegar

1 tsp brown sugar

1 bay leaf

½ tsp smoked paprika

½ tsp cracked black pepper

4 tbsp whisky

Bring a pan of salted water to the boil. Peel and roughly chop the potatoes, then cook for 15-20 minutes, until tender. Lift them out of the water, then mash with the butter and milk.

Add the diced swede to the same water you cooked the potatoes in and boil for 8 minutes, or until tender but still holding their shape. Drain, then fold into the potatoes along with the haggis. Season to taste with salt, pepper and a dash of Worcestershire sauce.

Wipe a work surface with a damp cloth and place a large sheet of cling film on top. Wipe smooth to remove any creases, then place another sheet of cling film on top and wipe again. Spoon the potato mixture along the centre and form into a sausage 3cm in diameter. Tightly wrap the sausage in cling film, tie both ends securely, then transfer to the freezer to set for 2 hours.

Meanwhile, make the ketchup. Fry the onion and garlic in the oil with a pinch of salt for 5 minutes, until soft. Add the tomatoes, vinegar, sugar, bay leaf and spices and leave to gently simmer for around 1 hour, stirring regularly.

Stir in the whisky a spoonful at a time until you're happy with the flavour. Leave to cool slightly, then discard the bay leaf and transfer the mixture to a blender. Blitz until smooth, then taste and check for seasoning. Reserve in the fridge until needed.

Use a serrated knife to cut the croquette mixture into 20 equal pieces, then pour the flour onto a plate, the eggs into a bowl and the breadcrumbs onto a tray. Dip each croquette in flour, then egg, then breadcrumbs, then in the egg and breadcrumbs again. Once they're all done, bring a deep pan of oil to 180°C.

Working in batches, deep-fry the croquettes for 3-5 minutes, until golden brown all over. Drain on kitchen paper, season with salt and serve with the whisky ketchup for dipping.

Black garlic potato farls with lemon and anchovy butter

Farls – an Irish flatbread made with potatoes – are wonderfully simple to cook and the perfect medium for all manner of toppings. Here, they're given a striking colour and an umami-rich, molasses-like flavour thanks to black garlic, an incredible ingredient that makes its way into many a restaurant menu. Topped with anchovy and lemon butter, they're a seriously moreish snack for almost any occasion.

Makes 12 farls
Cooking time: 1 hour 30 minutes
Equipment: 7cm round cutter

Farls

350g of floury potatoes, such as Maris Pipers

20 black garlic cloves

30g of unsalted butter, softened

75g of plain flour, plus extra for dusting

½ tsp baking powder

Olive oil, for frying

Anchovy butter

50g of unsalted butter, softened

10g of tinned anchovy fillets, drained and chopped

5g of flat-leaf parsley, chopped

1 lemon, zested

Bring a pan of salted water to the boil. Peel and roughly chop the potatoes, then add them to the water and cook for 15-20 minutes, until tender. Drain and leave in the colander for 5 minutes to steam-dry, then whilst still hot pass through a potato ricer or fine sieve to achieve a smooth, dry mash.

Use a pestle and mortar or the flat side of a knife to mash the black garlic cloves to a smooth paste, then stir through the butter. Mix this into the mashed potatoes until evenly dark brown throughout. Be careful not to overmix, as this will make the potatoes gluey. Season to taste with salt, then fold in the flour and baking powder until just combined.

Dust a work surface with flour and tip the dough out onto it. Roll out until 1.5cm thick, then use a 7cm round cutter to stamp out 12 farls. Place on a baking tray lined with baking paper and transfer to the fridge for half an hour to firm up.

While the farls sit in the fridge, mix together all the ingredients for the anchovy butter with a pinch of salt and set aside.

To cook the farls, place a large non-stick frying pan over a medium-high heat and add a splash of olive oil. Working in batches, add the farls and fry for around 3 minutes each side, adding a little more oil as needed. They're ready when both sides have started to crisp up slightly.

To serve, spread the farls generously with the anchovy butter. Transfer to serving plates and enjoy warm.

Chicken wings with Alabama sauce

Alabama sauce is a dip or glaze used with aplomb in the US state's thriving barbecue scene. Originally created in the 1920s, it takes mayonnaise and amps up the flavour with horseradish, sugar, vinegar and a hint of spice to create a sauce-dip-marinade hybrid that works particularly well with chicken. Here it's used to glaze wings that have been coated in a spice rub and left to dry out overnight for extra-crispy results.

Serves 6
Cooking time: 1 hour
plus overnight marinating time

Chicken

1kg of chicken wings

1 tsp dark muscovado sugar

½ tsp smoked paprika

½ tsp onion powder

½ tsp garlic powder

1 lemon, zested

¼ bunch of chives, finely chopped, to garnish

Alabama sauce

25g of mayonnaise

1 tsp cider vinegar

10g of light brown sugar

½ garlic clove, grated

¼ tsp horseradish sauce

¼ tbsp Worcestershire sauce

1 dash of Tabasco, or to taste

Celery salt, to taste

Begin by preparing the chicken wings. Pat them dry, then pull them at each end to stretch them out. Using a sharp knife, remove and discard the wing tip (the smallest end that looks a little like a feather), then cut the remaining wing into two pieces at the joint. You should be left with a small drumstick-shaped piece (a 'drumette') and an even smaller part known as a 'flat'. Repeat with the remaining wings.

Mix together the sugar, paprika, onion powder, garlic powder and lemon zest, then add a pinch of salt and pepper to create a rub. Toss the prepared wings in the rub until they're fully coated, then place on a wire rack. Place the rack on a tray then transfer to the fridge, uncovered, and leave overnight – this will ensure the skin on the wings is very dry when it comes to cooking them, resulting in a super-crispy exterior.

The next day, preheat an oven to 180°C. Transfer the wire rack and tray into the oven and cook the wings for 30 minutes, turning them halfway through.

While the wings cook, prepare the sauce. Simply mix all the ingredients together, seasoning with celery salt and freshly ground black pepper to taste.

After 30 minutes, take the wings out of the oven and liberally brush the wings with the Alabama sauce. Return the wings to the oven for a final 20 minutes, then serve hot sprinkled with chives and any remaining sauce on the side for dipping.

Seared salmon with porcini ponzu
by *Masaki Sugisaki*

Ponzu is a popular sauce in Japanese cuisine, combining the savoury flavours of soy and dried seaweed with the zesty tang of citrus juice. Chef Masaki Sugisaki's recipe shows you how to make it at home with an extra hit of umami from the dried mushrooms, which is then used to dress lightly seared wafer-thin slices of salmon. The ponzu is also equally good when used to dress beef carpaccio.

Serves 4
Cooking time: 1 hour

Salmon

½ banana shallot, finely chopped

200g of salmon fillet, skinned and as fresh as possible

100g of grapeseed oil, or vegetable oil

¼ bunch of chives, finely chopped

Micro coriander, or baby rocket, to garnish

Pink peppercorns, to garnish

Porcini ponzu

7g of dried porcini mushrooms

100g of rice vinegar

50g of light soy sauce

25g of lemon juice

10g of lime juice

20g of mirin

1 piece of kombu seaweed (optional)

Quickly rinse the dried porcini mushrooms in cold water to remove any dirt, then place in a bowl with the rest of the ponzu ingredients. Set aside at room temperature to infuse for 20 minutes.

Strain the mushrooms with a fine sieve set over a bowl to collect the liquid (discarding the kombu, if used), then squeeze any excess liquid from the mushrooms into the bowl – this liquid is your ponzu sauce. Chop the mushrooms as finely as possible, then set aside.

Place the chopped shallot in a bowl of cold water for 5 minutes to remove its astringency, then drain and set aside. Meanwhile, slice the salmon as thinly as possible – you ideally want each slice to be 2mm thick. It is much easier to do this when the salmon is fridge-cold, so keep it in the fridge until ready to slice. Arrange the slices onto serving dishes with a shallow rim.

Pour the grapeseed or vegetable oil into a small saucepan and place over a high heat. When it begins to smoke, very carefully spoon the oil over the salmon, trying to cover as much of the surface as possible – this will very lightly sear the exterior but leave it fresh and raw underneath. You may need to add a few tablespoons of oil to the salmon to sear it, so wipe away any excess with a cloth.

To serve, spoon the ponzu over the salmon until it is just covered (any remaining ponzu can be served on the side, or it will keep in the fridge for up to 2 weeks). Garnish with the chopped shallot, porcini and chives, then finish with some leaves and pink peppercorns.

Char siu pork neck with sweet chilli sauce
by Luke French

Pork neck is an incredible cut – affordable, full of flavour and bold enough to stand up against fierce cooking and strong spices. Rather than slow-cooking it until it falls apart, chef Luke French cures the meat before barbecuing over a high heat. The addition of rice koji in the curing mixture really helps to tenderise the pork, so it's well worth seeking out and experimenting with.

Serves 6-8
Cooking time: 2 hours 30 minutes
plus overnight curing time
Equipment: Meat thermometer

1kg of pork neck, any skin and excess fat removed

Curing mixture
25g of table salt
15g of smoked sea salt
50g of brown sugar
8g of Chinese five-spice
10g of chicken bouillon powder
12g of rice koji
1 tsp garlic powder
½ tsp onion powder
¼ tsp smoked paprika
¼ tsp chilli flakes
¼ tsp ground white pepper
3 Sichuan peppercorns, crushed
3 black peppercorns, ideally Telicherry, crushed

Sweet chilli sauce
40ml of rice vinegar
85g of caster sugar
1 tsp fish sauce
2 makrut lime leaves
1 red chilli, finely chopped
½ garlic clove, finely chopped
5 coriander stalks, finely chopped
1 tsp ginger, finely chopped
1 tsp cornflour
1 tbsp water

Combine all the ingredients for the curing mixture in a bowl and mix until fully incorporated. Place the pork in a container then pack the mixture all over the meat, ensuring it is fully covered. Cover and place in the fridge to cure for 24 hours.

The next day, wash off the curing mixture then pat the pork dry. Return it to the fridge uncovered for at least an hour to help dry out the exterior.

Light a barbecue. You could also use a heavy cast-iron frying pan over a high heat, but the barbecue will produce the best results. Preheat an oven to 200°C too, unless you have a barbecue which can be used to cook indirectly.

Once the barbecue (or pan) is searing hot, add the pork and cook, turning often, until very dark and blackened all over. This should take around 20 minutes, depending on the temperature of your barbecue.

Transfer the pork to a wire rack over a baking dish, then into the oven (or set up your barbecue for indirect cooking, adding some wood chips if you have them). Cook for 30-40 minutes, or until a thermometer inserted into the pork reads 50°C.

While the pork finishes cooking, make the sweet chilli sauce. Place all the ingredients apart from the cornflour and water into a saucepan with a pinch of salt and simmer for a few minutes, stirring regularly. Mix together the cornflour and water to make a slurry, then pour this into the sauce and whisk until thickened. Remove from the heat and set aside.

Once the pork has finished cooking, leave to rest for 10 minutes covered loosely with foil. To serve, slice the pork finely against the grain and divide between serving plates. Finish by dressing the meat in the sweet chilli sauce.

Patatas Bravísimas
by Angel Zapata Martin

Patatas bravas is the poster child for Spanish tapas, combining crisp deep-fried potatoes with a rich tomato sauce and punchy garlic allioli. Chef Angel Zapata Martin's version simply cannot be beaten – while this will technically make enough for four people, we can guarantee you'll be left wanting more. Both the allioli and bravas sauce can be made in advance and kept in the fridge for up to three days.

Serves 4
Cooking time: 1 hour 45 minutes
Equipment: Blender

Potatoes

4 large floury potatoes

Vegetable oil, for deep-frying

Allioli

1 garlic bulb

1 dash of olive oil

1 garlic clove

2 egg yolks

250ml of pomace oil, or a mixture of olive and vegetable oil

½ bunch of parsley, chopped

Brava sauce

375g of plum tomatoes

50ml of extra virgin olive oil, ideally arbequina, plus 3 tbsp extra for frying

½ bunch of spring onions, roughly chopped

2 garlic cloves

2 dried chillies, rehydrated in hot water then drained

1 choricero dried pepper, rehydrated in hot water then drained (optional)

¼ red pepper, roughly chopped

20ml of honey

60ml of cider vinegar

20g of plain flour

½ tsp tomato purée

100ml of chicken stock

Preheat an oven to 165°C. For the allioli, slice the garlic bulb in half along its equator, drizzle with olive oil and sprinkle with salt. Tightly wrap in foil and roast in the oven for 1 hour.

Meanwhile, make the brava sauce. Place the tomatoes in a blender and blitz until smooth. Add 2 tablespoons of olive oil to a pan over a low heat, then add the blended tomatoes. Cook, stirring often, for 30 minutes or until reduced by a third.

Add the olive oil, spring onions, garlic cloves, dried chillies, choricero pepper (if using) and red pepper to the blender. Blitz to a paste, then add to a separate saucepan with a dash more oil. Place over a medium heat and cook for 5 minutes, then stir in the honey and vinegar. Add the flour then cook for 2 minutes, before adding the tomato purée, chicken stock and reduced blitzed tomatoes. Simmer for 30 minutes, then blitz until smooth once more. Season with salt and set aside.

Once the garlic bulb has finished roasting, squeeze the soft cloves out of their skins into the blender. Add the raw garlic and egg yolks and blitz to a paste, then with the motor still running gradually drizzle in the oil until emulsified. Season with a pinch of salt and add most of the parsley (reserving some to garnish). Transfer to a piping bag or squeezy bottle if you have one and reserve in the fridge until needed.

Around 30 minutes before you plan to serve, heat a deep pan of vegetable oil to 150°C. Peel the potatoes then 'chip' them into bite-size pieces by cutting into the potato then twisting the blade – this creates shards of potato which will become extra-crisp. Working in batches, fry the potatoes for around 8 minutes, until soft inside and crisp on the outside. Drain on kitchen paper and sprinkle with salt.

To serve, divide the potatoes between bowls and top with the brava sauce. Pipe over the allioli then garnish with parsley.

Sharing Platters

Panzanella with avocado yoghurt and charred mackerel

Panzanella is an incredible Italian salad which sees hunks of stale bread rehydrated with a dressing of tomato juices and oil. Here, it's served with blistered mackerel fillets and a soothing avocado yoghurt. The quality of your tomatoes are the key to the success of this dish, so try to include a variety of different types and colours if possible. You can also swap out the mackerel for sardines or any other oily fish you like.

Serves 6
Cooking time: 30 minutes
Equipment: Blender

Panzanella

500g of heirloom tomatoes

1 small red onion, finely sliced into half-moons

150g of stale ciabatta, torn into bite-sized pieces

3 sprigs of oregano, leaves picked

1 tbsp sherry vinegar

1 tbsp extra virgin olive oil, plus extra for frying

1 tsp flaky sea salt

½ tsp freshly ground black pepper

6 mackerel fillets, pin-boned

Avocado yoghurt

2 large avocados

150g of plain yoghurt

1 lemon, juiced

Roughly chop the tomatoes into slices and wedges and place them in a large bowl along with any of the juices left on the board. Add the red onion, ciabatta and oregano leaves. Mix together the sherry vinegar, olive oil, salt and pepper then pour over the salad, tossing to combine. Set aside to marinate whilst you prepare the other elements.

Scoop out the avocado flesh and add to a blender with the yoghurt. Blitz until smooth, then season to taste with salt and lemon juice.

To cook the mackerel, you'll either need a frying pan or a barbecue – whichever you use, make sure they are very hot before you add the fish.

Lightly oil and season the skin side of the mackerel fillets then place them skin-side down in the pan or on the grill. Cook for around 5 minutes until blistered and crisp, then flip them over and cook for a few seconds more. Remove from the heat.

To serve, simply bring the salad, yoghurt and fish to the table so everyone can help themselves.

Yellow romesco with farinata, nectarines, potatoes and broccoli

Romesco – a Spanish sauce full of smoky, sweet and rich flavours – is the focal point for this platter of grilled fruits and vegetables, with slices of farinata (a thick savoury pancake made with chickpea flour) adding an extra contrast in texture. If the weather's nice then it's a great dish to cook on the barbecue, and a little crumbled feta over the top is a welcome addition if you don't need to keep things vegan. You could also use a slice of gluten-free bread in the sauce to cater for coeliacs, too.

Serves 6
Cooking time: 1 hour 45 minutes
plus resting time
Equipment: Blender

Farinata

150g of gram flour

300ml of water

½ tsp baking powder

4 tbsp olive oil

2 tbsp rosemary leaves, finely chopped

Pickled shallots

50ml of red wine vinegar

50ml of water

1 tbsp caster sugar

1 banana shallot, finely sliced into rings

Romesco sauce

6 yellow peppers

4 tbsp olive oil

2 slices of white bread

40g of blanched hazelnuts, toasted

2 tbsp sherry vinegar

4 garlic cloves, roughly chopped

½ lemon, juiced

Begin by making the farinata batter, as this needs an hour to rest (and could also be made the day before and kept in the fridge, if desired). Whisk together the flour, water, baking powder, 2 tablespoons of the olive oil and the chopped rosemary. Season the mixture with salt and pepper then cover and leave to rest for at least 1 hour.

For the shallots, place the vinegar, water, sugar and a pinch of salt into a small saucepan and heat until the sugar has dissolved. Take off the heat and add the shallot rings. Set aside.

Preheat a grill to high. Coat the peppers in 2 tablespoons of the olive oil and place on a tray. Sprinkle with salt then place under the grill and leave to blacken, turning the peppers until the skins are blistered and charred all over (around 20 minutes). Transfer to a heatproof lidded container or a bowl covered with cling film and leave until cool enough to handle. Turn off the grill and preheat the oven to 180°C.

Place the new potatoes in an oven tray and toss with olive oil, salt, pepper and the thyme leaves. Roast in the oven for 45 minutes or until cooked through and starting to crisp up.

When the peppers have cooled, peel and discard the black skins, stalks and seeds. Place the flesh in a blender along with the rest of the romesco ingredients then blend until smooth – you may need to add a little water to help loosen the mixture if needed. Taste and adjust the seasoning with more salt, pepper and sherry vinegar if needed. Set aside.

Ingredients continue overleaf   *Recipe continues overleaf*

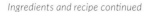

Ingredients and recipe continued

Salad

Olive oil, for drizzling

500g of small new potatoes, halved

2 sprigs of thyme, leaves picked, plus extra for garnishing

400g of Tenderstem broccoli

1 pinch of chilli flakes

4 nectarines, destoned and sliced into wedges

1 handful of smoked or salted almonds, roughly chopped

To cook the farinata, whisk the batter again as the flour will have settled at the bottom. Pour the remaining 2 tablespoons of oil into a high-sided round tray approx. 21cm in diameter and place in the oven to heat up.

Once the oil is hot, pour in the batter and swirl around to cover the tray – it should be around 1-2cm high. Cook in the oven for 25 minutes alongside the potatoes.

Meanwhile, place a griddle pan over a high heat. Whilst you wait for it to get hot, toss the broccoli with a little olive oil and a pinch of chilli flakes. Cook on the griddle until charred, then push to one side. Drizzle the nectarines with olive oil and griddle for about 2 minutes on each side to get nice bar marks.

Once the potatoes are cooked though and the pancake batter has set, remove both from the oven and turn on the grill. Once hot, place the farinata under it for a few minutes until golden and starting to crisp up on the top. Transfer to a chopping board and cut into slices.

To assemble the platter, place the romesco sauce in a bowl and garnish with a few thyme leaves. Arrange the roast potatoes, farinata, broccoli and nectarines on a larger serving dish (or 2 smaller ones) around it. Sprinkle over the pickled shallots and smoked almonds to finish, then bring it to the table with plates so everyone can help themselves.

Spatchcocked chicken with chicken fat mayo, lemony roast potatoes and green beans

While a spatchcocked chicken always catches the eye, the real star of the show in this dish is the potatoes, cooked underneath the bird so they can soak up all its delicious juices. Whisking some of the stock into the mayonnaise gives it some extra oomph, and the tomato green beans can be made in advance (they taste even better when made the day before and are served at room temperature).

Serves 4-6
Cooking time: 1 hour 30 minutes

Chicken

1 large, free-range chicken

1 tbsp olive oil

1 tsp dried thyme

1 tsp dried oregano

2 lemons

Mayonnaise

150g of mayonnaise

1 small garlic clove

Potatoes

6 large potatoes – a semi-waxy variety such as Desiree works well

150ml of chicken stock

50ml of extra virgin olive oil

4 garlic cloves, finely grated

2 sprigs of rosemary, leaves picked and chopped

Green beans

60ml of extra virgin olive oil

1 onion, finely diced

5 garlic cloves, finely chopped

1 tsp dried oregano

400g of green beans, trimmed

1 tin (400g) of chopped tomatoes

200ml of water

1 handful of parsley, chopped

1 handful of dill, chopped

Preheat an oven to 180°C. Peel the potatoes and cut into halves (or quarters if they're big). Place them in a large, deep baking tray then pour over the chicken stock and extra virgin olive oil. Stir in the grated garlic and rosemary, then set aside.

To spatchcock the chicken, place the bird breast-side down on a chopping board. Using a strong pair of scissors, cut along either side of the backbone and discard it. Trim away any excess skin or fat from around the neck, then flip the bird over and use the palm of your hand to flatten it.

Drizzle over the oil, then rub in the thyme, oregano and the zest of both lemons with plenty of salt and pepper. Cut the zested lemons in half and squeeze the juice over the potatoes, then throw the lemon halves in too. Place a wire rack over the potatoes, then sit the chicken on top. Transfer to the oven and cook for 50 minutes.

While the potatoes and chicken roast in the oven, prepare the beans. Heat the olive oil in a heavy-bottomed pan then add the onion with a pinch of salt. Gently cook, stirring regularly, until the onions have softened but not taken on any colour (around 5 minutes), then add the garlic and oregano and cook for a few more minutes.

Add the green beans to the pan and stir to combine, then add the tomatoes and water. Bring to a simmer then cook on a low heat for 45-60 minutes, until the sauce has reduced and is clinging to the beans. When ready, remove from the heat – they taste best when warm or at room temperature, so there's no need to reheat them.

Recipe continues overleaf

Recipe continued

Check the chicken is cooked by inserting a skewer into the thickest part of the thigh – if the juices run clear, it's ready. If they're still pink, then return it to the oven for another 10-20 minutes. Once cooked, lift the rack off the potatoes and cover the bird loosely with foil to rest for 20 minutes. Turn the oven up to 200°C.

Take a few tablespoons of the lemony chicken stock from the potatoes, trying to get as much of the fat floating on the top as you can, then whisk it into the mayonnaise. Grate in the garlic clove and season to taste with salt and pepper. Return the potatoes to the oven for another 20 minutes, until they take on some colour. They won't go fully crisp like regular roast potatoes because of the liquid, but they will taste far better!

When ready to serve, season the beans with salt and pepper then fold through the parsley and dill. Carve the chicken and serve with the potatoes, beans and mayonnaise.

Toulouse sausage-stuffed squid with spicy tomato orzo

Tender squid tubes are stuffed with herby sausage meat and served on a bed of orzo pasta and tomato sauce in this warming, hearty dish. If your squid come with tentacles, don't waste them – dust them in flour and flash-fry them in a searing hot pan for a minute or two, then nestle them into the sauce before serving.

Serves 4-6
Cooking time: 1 hour 30 minutes
Equipment: Cocktail sticks

Squid

4 large squid tubes, or 6 smaller ones, defrosted if frozen

600g of Toulouse sausages, or herbed sausages

150g of fresh breadcrumbs

2 tbsp black olive tapenade

1 red chilli, deseeded and finely chopped

1 lemon, zested

½ bunch parsley, chopped

Olive oil, for frying

Lemon wedges, to serve

Tomato orzo

2 tbsp extra virgin olive oil

6 garlic cloves, finely sliced

1 tsp chilli flakes

100ml of white wine

1 tin (400g) of chopped tomatoes

400g of passata

350g of orzo

½ bunch of parsley, chopped

Begin with the tomato sauce. Place a saucepan over a medium heat and add the olive oil. Once hot, add the sliced garlic and chilli flakes along with a pinch of salt. Cook for a few minutes until softened, then as soon as the garlic starts to colour add the wine. Bring to a simmer and cook until reduced by half. Add the tomatoes and passata and return to a simmer. Cook for 30 minutes, stirring occasionally.

While the sauce cooks, prepare the stuffing. Cut a slit into the sausages and discard the skins, then place the sausage meat in a bowl with the breadcrumbs, tapenade, chilli, lemon zest, parsley and a pinch of salt and pepper. Mix well until evenly distributed, then divide into 4 or 6 equal portions.

Stuff the squid tubes with the sausage meat mixture, then use cocktail sticks to secure the open end of the squid together – this is important as the squid will shrink as it cooks and the stuffing will fall out otherwise. Pat the squid dry and set aside.

Preheat an oven to 180°C. Transfer the tomato sauce to a deep ovenproof dish large enough to hold the squid and place a large non-stick frying pan over a high heat. When the pan is smoking hot, add a dash of oil and then the squid – be careful as the oil might spit a little. Cook for a minute or two on each side until golden, then nestle the squid into the tomato sauce. Transfer to the oven and cook for 30 minutes.

Bring a pan of salted water to the boil. When the squid have around 8 minutes of cooking time left, add the orzo to the water and cook for 8 minutes, or until al dente.

Remove the squid from the oven and carefully transfer them to a plate. Drain the orzo and stir it through the tomato sauce, along with two-thirds of the chopped parsley. Place the squid back on top of the sauce, then sprinkle with the remaining parsley. Serve with lemon wedges.

Harissa-roast salmon Niçoise

Nothing says summertime quite like a Niçoise salad, but this recipe takes things to the next level by replacing the tuna with tender flakes of salmon roasted in harissa, lemon and honey. The potatoes are lightly fried in cumin-infused butter, and the green beans are given a citric kick thanks to a scattering of sumac.

Serves 6
Cooking time: 45 minutes

Salmon

1 side of salmon, weighing approx. 800g, skin-on

1 tbsp harissa

1 tbsp olive oil

1 tsp honey

¼ lemon, juiced

¼ tsp cumin seeds

Salad

3 eggs

450g of new potatoes

25g of unsalted butter

1 tsp cumin seeds

200g of green beans

1 pinch of sumac

180g of cherry tomatoes, on the vine

50g of rocket

1 cos lettuce, washed and roughly chopped

80g of black olives

Extra virgin olive oil, for drizzling

Preheat an oven to 200°C and bring a large pan of salted water to the boil. For the salmon, place the fish skin-side down on a baking tray and mix together all the remaining ingredients with a pinch of salt. Pour the dressing all over the salmon, ensuring it is well coated, then place in the oven and cook for 25 minutes.

Meanwhile, carefully lower the eggs into the boiling water and cook for 6½ minutes. Drain and place under running cold water to cool whilst you bring another pan of salted water to the boil. Slice the potatoes into 1cm discs, then add to the water and cook for 10 minutes. Peel the eggs while the potatoes cook, then halve and set aside. When the potatoes are tender, drain.

Place a frying pan over a medium heat and add the butter. Once melted, add the cumin seeds – as soon as they begin to sizzle, tip in the potatoes. Toss to coat in the butter, season with salt and pepper and cook for a few minutes until the potatoes just start to colour. Turn off the heat.

Once the salmon is cooked, remove from the oven and set aside. Lower the heat to 180°C, toss the green beans with a little oil, sea salt and sumac, then place on a baking tray and roast for 5 minutes.

After 5 minutes, add the cherry tomatoes to the tray of beans and return to the oven for another 10 minutes, or until the skins have split but they are still holding their shape.

To serve, lightly dress the rocket and cos lettuce in a drizzle of oil, then arrange on a large serving platter (or 2 smaller platters). Gently flake the salmon into large chunks and arrange on top, along with the potatoes, beans and tomatoes. Finish with a scattering of olives and the halved eggs, with a pinch of salt and pepper and a final drizzle of oil.

Za'atar spiced lamb leg with hasselback courgettes and butter bean tahini dip

Delicately spiced and marinated lamb is cooked to blushing pink perfection in this wonderful Middle Eastern-inspired dish, alongside harissa-dressed blistered courgettes and a creamy butter bean dip. By 'hasselbacking' the courgettes, you allow all the flavours of the harissa to permeate the vegetable, making it soft and unctuous in the centre and crisp on the outside.

Serves 6-8
Cooking time: 1 hour 45 minutes
plus overnight marinating time
Equipment: Blender

Lamb

1 lamb leg, weighing approx. 1.5kg, butterflied

2 tbsp za'atar

1 lemon, juiced and zested

1 tbsp olive oil

Courgettes

4 courgettes

3 tsp harissa

4 tsp olive oil

Lemon juice, to taste

Dip

2 tins (800g) of butter beans, drained

2 garlic cloves, roughly chopped

2 tbsp tahini

200ml of water

1 lemon, juiced

Dukkah

3 tbsp chopped hazelnuts

1 tbsp sesame seeds

¼ tsp cumin seeds

¼ tsp coriander seeds

To serve

½ bunch of fresh coriander, chopped

Extra virgin olive oil, for drizzling

Flatbreads

Mix the za'atar, lemon juice and zest, olive oil and a pinch of salt together, then rub the mixture all over the lamb. Place in a container, cover and leave to marinate in the fridge overnight.

The next day, prepare the courgettes. Line a courgette up next to a wooden spoon – this will stop you from accidentally slicing all the way through the courgette. Make lots of little cuts along the courgette with around 5mm between each slice to create the 'hasselback' effect. Repeat with the remaining courgettes.

Mix together the harissa, olive oil and a squeeze of lemon juice, then season with a pinch of salt and pepper. Use a butter knife or small spatula to carefully massage this mixture into the slits of the courgettes – this takes a little time, but it's well worth it. Transfer the courgettes to a baking tray, reserving any leftover dressing to one side.

Preheat an oven to 200°C and place a large frying or griddle pan over a high heat. Once smoking hot, place the marinated lamb skin-side down in the pan and cook until caramelised and golden. Flip the lamb and continue searing until browned and crisp all over, then transfer to the oven and cook for 40 minutes. 10 minutes after the lamb has gone in, place the courgettes in the oven too.

While the lamb and courgettes, cook, make the dip. Place the drained butter beans in a blender with the garlic and tahini and blitz until smooth. Add the water to loosen (you may not need it all), then season to taste with plenty of salt and lemon juice.

Recipe continues overleaf

Recipe continued

To make the dukkah, place a small frying pan over a medium heat and toast the hazelnuts for 5 minutes, or until golden – make sure they don't burn or blacken as they will taste bitter. Tip them out into a bowl, then add the sesame, cumin and coriander seeds to the same pan and toast for a minute until they smell fragrant. Add them to the hazelnuts, then season with a pinch of salt and pepper.

After the lamb has been cooking for 40 minutes, take it out of the oven and leave to rest for 20 minutes (leave the courgettes in the oven to continue cooking).

To serve, slice the lamb against the grain and arrange on a serving platter alongside the courgettes (drizzling any remaining dressing over them as you do so). Place the butter bean dip into a serving bowl, then sprinkle with the dukkah and add a drizzle of olive oil. Finish with the coriander leaves and serve with flatbreads.

Pepper-crusted steak salad with celeriac, roast radishes and horseradish salad cream

The peppery flavours of radishes and watercress stand up against the intensity of rare flank steak (also known as bavette) in this colourful salad. With earthy celeriac wedges, a homemade horseradish salad cream and clever little Parmesan crisps to garnish, it's a showstopper of a dish to bring to the table. Serve with good bread to turn this into a do-it-yourself steak sandwich platter.

Serves 6
Cooking time: 1 hour

Steak

1kg of flank steak, cut into 7cm-wide strips

2 tbsp black peppercorns

2 tbsp pink peppercorns

2 tsp flaky sea salt

1 dash of vegetable oil

Celeriac and radishes

1 celeriac, weighing approx. 700g

3 tbsp olive oil

1 tbsp mustard seeds

200g of radishes, ideally in a variety of colours, trimmed

1 tsp honey

Salad

25g of Parmesan

80g of watercress

80g of rocket

1 bunch of dill, fronds picked

Horseradish salad cream

2 eggs

½ tsp sugar

1 tsp Dijon mustard

1 tbsp creamed horseradish

1 tbsp white wine vinegar

75ml olive oil

75ml double cream

1 dash of lemon juice

Crush the black and pink peppercorns in a pestle and mortar along with the flaky sea salt. Apply the mixture to the strips of steak, then set aside at room temperature to cure lightly.

Preheat an oven to 180°C. Peel and chop the celeriac into small wedges, then toss in 2 tablespoons of the olive oil, the mustard seeds and a pinch of salt and pepper. Spread the celeriac out across a baking tray and roast for 30-40 minutes, until browned round the edges.

Toss the radishes with the remaining oil and season. Add to a separate baking dish and set aside.

While the celeriac roasts, prepare the salad cream. Boil the eggs for 8 minutes, then run under cold water and peel. Discard the egg whites, leaving you with 2 hard-boiled yolks.

Using a fork, mash the yolks in a bowl until smooth, then add the sugar, mustard and horseradish, followed by the vinegar. Whilst whisking constantly, slowly drizzle in the oil to create an emulsion – if the mixture splits you can add a splash of water. Whisk in the cream, then season with lemon juice and salt. Pass through a fine sieve to remove any lumps and reserve in the fridge until needed.

After the celeriac has been roasting for 20 minutes, give the pan a shake. Place the radishes in the oven and cook for 10 minutes, or until they wrinkle up and start to turn translucent.

Recipe continues overleaf

Recipe continued

Meanwhile, line a small tray with baking paper and finely grate the Parmesan onto it in a thin, tight layer. Once the radishes have been roasting for 10 minutes, take them out and drizzle them with the honey, then return them to the oven. Place the Parmesan in the oven too and leave everything to cook for a final 5 minutes.

Place a large griddle or frying pan over a high heat and wait until it is smoking hot. Add a dash of oil, followed by the peppered steaks. Fry the steaks for 3 minutes on each side, then transfer to a plate and leave to rest for 5 minutes.

Dress the watercress and rocket with a tablespoon of the salad cream, then stir in the dill fronds. To serve, arrange the salad on a large platter (or 2 smaller ones) and sprinkle over the celeriac and radishes. Carve the steak against the grain into thin slices, then arrange these on top. Break the Parmesan crisps into shards and scatter over the platter, then bring to the table with the horseradish salad cream on the side.

Baja fish tacos with cucumber and pistachio salsa
by *Santiago Lastra*

This famous dish from Baja California is given a Santiago Lastra twist in this intriguing sharing dish. With Marmite in the batter, a salsa made from pistachios and cucumber, a smoky chipotle cream and crisp cabbage bolstered with juicy sauerkraut and fiery habanero, it's both familiar and new at the same time.

Makes 12 tacos
Cooking time: 1 hour
Equipment: Food processor

Fish

2 tsp Marmite (optional)

200ml of sparkling water

4 tbsp plain flour

4 tbsp masa harina

2 tsp baking powder

360g of pollack fillet, or any white fish

Sunflower oil, for deep-frying

Rice flour, for dusting

Chipotle cream

4 tbsp chipotle paste

8 tsp double cream

8 tsp mayonnaise

Salsa

1 garlic clove, unpeeled

1 serrano chilli

50g of shelled pistachios

1 small onion, roughly chopped

½ cucumber, deseeded and chopped

6 mint leaves, finely chopped

10 coriander leaves, finely chopped

2 lemons, juiced

To serve

200g of red cabbage, finely sliced

200g of white cabbage, finely sliced

4 tsp sauerkraut

1 habanero chilli, sliced

12 small flour tortillas

Make the chipotle cream by mixing all the ingredients together. Cover and reserve in the fridge until needed.

Dissolve the Marmite (if using) into the sparkling water, then whisk in the flour, masa harina, baking powder and a pinch of salt. Cover and set aside.

For the salsa, place the garlic clove and serrano chilli in a dry frying pan and toast for 5-10 minutes until blackened all over. Leave until cool enough to handle, then peel the garlic and remove the stem and seeds from the chilli.

Place the pistachios in a food processor and blitz to a powder, then add the toasted garlic and serrano chilli along with the onion, cucumber, mint, coriander and lemon juice. Pulse a few times to create a bright green chunky sauce, adding a little oil to loosen if needed, then season to taste with salt. Set aside.

Heat a large, deep pan of sunflower oil to 170°C. Meanwhile, cut the fish into 12 equal pieces, then dust with the rice flour and give the batter a quick whisk as it may have separated. Once the oil is hot, dip the fish in the batter and deep-fry for 3 minutes, or until the batter is golden and crisp (work in batches if needed). Drain on kitchen paper and set aside.

To serve, mix together the cabbages, sauerkraut and habanero chilli with a pinch of salt in a serving dish and heat up the tortillas in a dry frying pan. Bring both to the table along with the fish, chipotle cream and salsa for everyone to help themselves to.

Salad leaves with crispy chicken skin and a duo of dressings
by Harriet Mansell

More of a blueprint than a strict recipe, Harriet Mansell's sharing salad isn't just nice to look at – it's a masterclass in contrasting flavours and textures. The sweet sourness of the fermented dressing contrasts with the creamy richness of the tahini, while crispy chicken skin (or yeast, to make the dish vegetarian) adds savoury crunch. Don't be afraid to hide any pickles you happen to have amongst the greenery too.

Serves 4
Cooking time: 30 minutes
plus 2 weeks fermenting time

Salad

2 chicken skins, or 4 tbsp nutritional yeast flakes

4 handfuls of the best quality mixed salad leaves you can find

1 bunch of soft herbs, such as dill, coriander or basil

Edible flowers, to garnish

Fermented fruit dressing

50g of rhubarb, or other seasonal fruit like strawberries or plums, sliced

100g of local honey

Malt tahini dressing

3 tbsp tahini

1 tbsp cold-pressed rapeseed oil

½ garlic clove, finely grated

1 tsp sea salt

Malt vinegar, as needed

The fermented dressing takes 2 weeks to develop in flavour, so begin with this. Simply place the sliced fruit in a jar or container and cover in honey, ensuring the fruit is fully submerged. Seal and leave at room temperature for 2 weeks.

Preheat an oven to 180°C and line a baking tray with baking paper. Scrape any excess fat off the chicken skins, then lay them flat on the tray. Bake in the oven for 10-15 minutes, until golden and crisp (do not allow them to turn dark or burn as they will taste bitter). Leave to cool slightly, then chop into shards and reserve in an airtight container until needed. If you're using yeast flakes, then dress them lightly in smoked rapeseed oil and a pinch of salt and roast in the oven for 5-10 minutes, stirring occasionally, until golden.

For the tahini dressing, mix the tahini, rapeseed oil, garlic and salt together in a bowl until smooth. Add a good glug of the malt vinegar, along with a few tablespoons of cold water and a pinch of pepper. Mix until smooth, adding a little more water if it's still too thick, then taste. Adjust the flavour by adding more salt and vinegar – you want it as vinegary and salty as you can take it. If the dressing splits, it's because the water you added wasn't cold enough; blitzing in an ice cube with a stick blender should save it.

To assemble the salad, reserve some of the prettiest salad leaves to one side with the edible flowers. Begin layering up the other leaves in a salad bowl, nestling in the soft herbs as you go. Arrange the reserved leaves and edible flowers on top, then garnish with the chicken skin or yeast. Bring the salad to the table with the 2 dressings on the side so everyone can admire your picture-perfect arrangement, then drizzle over the tahini and liquid from the fermented fruit and toss everything together to dress.

Steamed mussels with pistachio, lemon and chilli pangrattato
by Ben Tish

Mussels are steamed in a fresh, fragrant broth of wine, lemon, chilli and mint in Ben Tish's Sicilian-inspired dish. The pangrattato – a mixture of fried breadcrumbs, pistachios and Parmesan – adds a nutty, colourful crunch to the plump, sweet mussels. Try tossing some al dente pasta through the mussels to make the dish more substantial and transport yourself to the southern Italian island.

Serves 4
Cooking time: 20 minutes

Pangrattato

Extra virgin olive oil, for frying

1 large handful of stale breadcrumbs

100g of shelled pistachios, as green as you can find, roughly chopped

50g of Parmesan, finely grated

Mussels

1kg of live mussels

250ml of dry white wine

1 lemon, juiced and zested

2 small red chillies, deseeded and finely chopped

100g of unsalted butter, diced

1 handful of mint leaves, roughly chopped

To make the pangrattato, place a frying pan over a medium heat and add a generous glug of olive oil. Add the breadcrumbs and fry for 3-5 minutes, or until golden brown. Stir in the pistachios and Parmesan, then set aside.

Clean the mussels by removing any hairy fibres from the shells then give them a good wash and rinse in running water. Discard any open mussels that don't close when firmly tapped.

Place a large lidded saucepan or casserole dish over a high heat and throw in the mussels, white wine, lemon juice and zest and chilli. Cover and cook for 5 minutes, shaking the pan regularly, or until the mussels start to open up. If any remain shut after giving them a firm tap, discard them.

Add the butter along with a good pinch of freshly ground black pepper and stir through. Scatter the mint leaves over the top along with the pangrattato and bring to the table.

Al Fresco

Coronation egg sandwiches

The flavours of coronation chicken – curried mayonnaise with juicy sultanas – are applied to the classic egg mayo in these perfect little sandwiches, complete with a sprinkling of Bombay mix for crunch. The homemade buns are known as Japanese milk bread, a brioche-style recipe that's fantastic for all manner of fillings that begins life as a roux-like starter for added richness.

Makes 6
Cooking time: 1 hour
plus proving time
Equipment: Stand mixer

Buns

175g of whole milk

35g of double cream

190g of bread flour

10g of caster sugar

1 tsp sea salt

7g of fresh yeast, or 3g of dried yeast

40g of unsalted butter, softened

1 egg, beaten

1 tbsp onion seeds

Filling

6 large eggs

2 tbsp mayonnaise

2 tbsp natural yoghurt

1 tbsp mango chutney

1 tbsp Madras curry powder

½ tsp turmeric powder

4 spring onions, finely chopped

3 tbsp sultanas

1 lemon, juiced

½ bunch of coriander, chopped

½ bunch of mint, chopped

1 red chilli, deseeded and finely sliced

6 handfuls of Bombay mix

The buns take around 3 hours to prove and bake, so begin with these. Measure out 60g of the whole milk and add to a pan with the double cream. Bring to a simmer, then whisk in 15g of the bread flour. Cook, stirring constantly, until the mixture forms a roux-type consistency and becomes to come away from the sides of the pan. It will be lumpy at first, but the lumps should disappear with rigorous stirring. Remove from the heat and leave to cool.

Set up a stand mixer with a dough hook attachment. Add the remaining bread flour, sugar, salt and yeast to the bowl along with the cooled starter. Mix on a low speed to combine, then gradually add the remaining whole milk. Mix until combined, then cover and set aside for 20 minutes. After this time, the dough should be very elastic and wet.

Start the motor again on a low speed, then gradually add little pinches of the butter, waiting until they are incorporated before adding more. The dough will become smoother and less sticky. Once all the butter is incorporated, turn the speed up and continue to mix until the dough starts slapping against the sides of the bowl (around 5 minutes). Cover the bowl with a damp tea towel and place somewhere warm for 1 hour, or until doubled in size.

Tip the dough out onto a lightly oiled work surface and knock it back by punching and pressing it with your hands. Knead a little more to ensure it's all well combined, then divide into 6 equal portions. Use a cupped hand to roll each portion against the work surface into a tight ball, trying to keep the seam at the bottom. Place the buns onto a tray lined with baking paper, cover loosely with a damp tea towel and leave to prove for another 30-45 minutes. Meanwhile, preheat an oven to 160°C.

Recipe continues overleaf

Recipe continued

Gently brush each bun liberally with the beaten egg then sprinkle with onion seeds. Bake for 20 minutes, then set aside to cool.

While the buns bake, bring a pan of water to the boil. Gently lower the eggs in and cook for 8 minutes, then run them under cold water to cool. Peel and roughly chop the eggs (leaving some larger chunks in there for texture), then place in a bowl.

Mix together the mayonnaise, yoghurt, chutney, curry powder, turmeric, spring onions, sultanas and a squeeze of lemon juice. Carefully fold through the chopped eggs, ensuring everything is completely combined but the eggs aren't broken down too much. Season to taste with salt, pepper and more lemon juice if needed.

To serve, slice the buns in half and lightly toast them. Fill generously with the egg mixture, then top with some fresh herbs, sliced chilli and Bombay mix.

Ham hock terrine with chive scones and mustard mayonnaise

Terrines are something chefs obsess over in the kitchen and offer plenty of opportunities to experiment with flavour combinations to suit your own tastes. This recipe sees slow-cooked ham hock paired with apricot and herbs to create a fantastic filling for cheesy scones, slathered with a homemade mustard mayo.

Serves 8-10
Cooking time: 1 hour 45 minutes
plus 3 hours simmering time and overnight setting time
Equipment: Food processor, 7cm round cutter

Terrine

1 ham hock, weighing approx. 1.6kg

1 onion, roughly chopped

2 carrots, roughly chopped

2 celery sticks, roughly chopped

1 tsp black peppercorns

2 bay leaves

¼ bunch of thyme

2 gelatine leaves

1 banana shallot, finely diced

60g of dried apricots, chopped

1 bunch of chives, finely chopped

1 bunch of parsley, finely chopped

2 tsp apple cider vinegar

Scones

450g of self-raising flour, plus extra for dusting

1 tbsp baking powder

1 tsp sea salt

120g of unsalted butter

150g of cheddar, finely grated

3 tbsp chopped chives

350ml of whole milk

1 egg, beaten

Ingredients continue overleaf

Begin by making the terrine a day in advance. Place the ham hock in a large saucepan and cover with cold water. Bring to the boil, then pour away the water to remove any impurities. Cover the ham hock with fresh water and add the vegetables, peppercorns, bay leaves and thyme. Bring to a simmer, then cover and cook for 3 hours, until the ham is very tender. Lift out the hock and set aside to cool. Strain the cooking liquid and measure out 400ml.

Give the saucepan a quick wash, then pour the measured 400ml of stock back into it. Simmer until reduced by half, then turn the heat down to low and keep warm. Meanwhile, pull the ham hock meat off the bone and place in a mixing bowl – you want it in small pieces rather than completely shredded.

Soak the gelatine leaves in cold water for 5 minutes to soften. Meanwhile, add the diced shallot, apricots, chives and parsley to the ham. Squeeze the gelatine leaves to drain then add them to the warm stock, stirring until dissolved. Pour the stock into the bowl with the meat, add the vinegar, season with salt and pepper and give everything a final stir. At this point you can either place the terrine in a mould lined with cling film, or roll it into a sausage shape tightly wrapped in cling film – you ideally want the sausage to be around 6cm in diameter. Place in the fridge to set overnight.

The next day, make the scones. Place the flour, baking powder, salt and butter in a food processor and pulse to a sandy consistency. Add the chives and three-quarters of the cheese, then pulse until just mixed. Add the milk bit by bit, continuing to pulse, until a dough comes together (you may not need all the milk). Shape the dough into a ball, place in a bowl and cover with a tea towel. Leave to rest for 20 minutes. Meanwhile, preheat an oven to 180°C.

Recipe continues overleaf

Ingredients and recipe continued

Mustard mayonnaise

2 egg yolks

1 tbsp wholegrain mustard

1 tsp mustard powder

200ml of vegetable oil

Lemon juice, to taste

Once rested, tip the dough out onto a lightly floured work surface and roll out to around 3.5cm thick. Use a 7cm round cutter to stamp out 8-10 scones. Transfer the scones to a baking tray lined with baking paper, then brush the tops of them with the beaten egg and sprinkle over the remaining cheese. Bake for 8-10 minutes, or until golden on top.

While the scones bake, make the mayonnaise by blitzing the eggs, wholegrain mustard and mustard powder in a food processor until pale and smooth. With the motor still running, gradually pour in the vegetable oil until emulsified. If it begins to split, add a splash of cold water. Season to taste with salt and lemon juice.

To serve, ensure the terrine has come to room temperature before slicing. Slice the scones in half, spread liberally with the mustard mayonnaise and add a puck of terrine.

Prawns in saor

Sarde in saor is a Venetian dish which marinates fried sardines in a pickle liquor full of sweet onions, garlic, raisins and pine nuts. This recipe replaces the sardines with fat, juicy prawns for a luxurious twist – it's also great for entertaining as it can be made entirely in advance.

Serves 6
Cooking time: 35 minutes
plus marinating time

Prawns

350g of raw king prawns, peeled

30g of plain flour

2 tbsp extra virgin olive oil

Crusty bread, to serve

Saor

1 large white onion, very finely sliced
(use a mandoline if you have one)

4 tbsp extra virgin olive oil

2 garlic cloves, very finely sliced

1 bay leaf

2 sprigs of thyme

50ml of white wine

50ml of water

30ml of white wine vinegar

1 tsp caster sugar

2 tbsp raisins

2 tbsp pine nuts

Place the onion, oil, garlic, bay leaf, thyme and a pinch of salt in a frying pan over a very low heat and gently cook for 15-20 minutes, until soft but without colour. Take your time as you need to bring all the sweetness out of the onions without browning them.

Add the wine, water, vinegar and sugar and bring to a simmer, then continue to cook until reduced by one-third. Add the raisins and pine nuts, then remove from the heat. Season with a pinch of salt and pepper, then leave to cool.

Dust the prawns in the flour and a pinch of salt and pepper. Place a frying pan over a high heat and add half the oil. Once hot, add half the prawns, then cook for a minute each side until pink and slightly crisp. Transfer to a deep dish, then repeat with the remaining prawns and oil.

Pour the sweet and sour onion mixture over the prawns and leave to marinate in the fridge for at least 1 hour, but ideally overnight. To serve, bring the mixture out of the fridge for 30 minutes to come to room temperature. Divide between plates with a few slices of crusty bread.

Crab pâté with tarragon and pink grapefruit

Crab always brings a little luxury to proceedings and this foolproof pâté can be made well in advance ready for when friends come round for a drink in the garden. Experiment with different citrus fruits, herbs or other flavourings to suit your own tastes.

Serves 6
Cooking time: 30 minutes
plus setting time

200g of crab meat, a mix of white and brown

3 tbsp crème fraîche

3 large egg yolks

2 dashes of Tabasco

3 dashes of Worcestershire sauce

3 sprigs of tarragon, leaves picked and chopped

1 pink grapefruit

120g of unsalted butter

Good bread, to serve

Place the crab meat and crème fraîche in a saucepan over a low heat. Once warm (but not hot), add the egg yolks then cook for 5 minutes, stirring regularly, until the mixture thickens slightly and is completely combined. Remove from the heat.

Season the mixture with salt and pepper, then add the Tabasco, Worcestershire sauce and tarragon. Zest half of the pink grapefruit into the mixture, then transfer to serving ramekins or bowls. You could also set the mixture in 1 large sharing bowl.

Top and tail the zested grapefruit, then carefully cut away the peel, removing as much white pith as possible. Cut out two segments of the grapefruit, again avoiding any white pith, then set aside.

Place the butter in a small saucepan and heat until it turns brown and nutty. Strain through a fine sieve into a bowl to remove any larger milk solids, then add the grapefruit segments and stir until they break apart into individual pearls. Add a pinch of salt, leave to cool for around 5 minutes, then pour the butter over each ramekin of crab. Transfer to the fridge and leave to set for at least 1 hour.

Take the pâtés out of the fridge around 30 minutes before serving to allow them to come to room temperature. Enjoy with slices of bread, toasted if desired.

Smoked trout and spinach roulade

An easy make-ahead dish that sings with the flavours of an English country garden, this savoury roulade contains a creamy smoked trout filling and a verdant spinach and herb sponge. Pretty to look at, but even better to eat.

Serves 6-8
Cooking time: 45 minutes
plus cooling time
**Equipment: Blender,
electric whisk**

300g of spinach

50g of soft herbs, such as dill, tarragon and basil

5 medium eggs, separated

30g of plain flour

1 tsp baking powder

2 fillets of hot-smoked trout, or hot-smoked salmon, weighing approx. 180g

250g of full-fat cream cheese

1 lemon, zested and juiced

Toasted flaked almonds, to serve (optional)

Place the spinach in a wide frying pan over a high heat and cover with a lid. Cook for a minute or 2, stirring occasionally, until the spinach has completely wilted and the water is starting to evaporate. Spread the spinach out onto a plate to cool quickly, then squeeze out as much liquid as you can, a handful at a time. Finely chop the leaves, along with the herbs, then set aside.

Preheat an oven to 180°C and line a large baking tray that's around 35x30cm in size with baking paper. Add the egg yolks to a blender with the flour, baking powder and a large pinch of salt. Blitz to a paste, then add the spinach and herbs. Blitz again until smooth and bright green, then transfer to a bowl.

Use an electric whisk to whisk the egg whites to stiff peaks. Carefully fold the egg whites into the spinach mixture, trying to keep as much air in the whites as possible. Pour the mixture onto the lined tray, smoothing it down if needed – it should be 2-3cm in depth. Bake for 12 minutes.

Meanwhile, make the filling. Flake the trout into a bowl then stir in the cream cheese, lemon zest and a generous amount of black pepper. Season to taste with salt and lemon juice.

Flip the baked sponge out onto a wire rack and carefully peel off the baking paper. Leave to cool, then flip the sponge over again and spread the trout filling on top in an even layer. Roll up the roulade, starting at the bottom and rolling it away from you. You want to roll it up along its longest edge.

To serve, trim the ends off the roulade then cut into 6-8 slices. Serve scattered with toasted flaked almonds if desired.

Spiced lamb cigars with sumac and cucumber yoghurt

They might look like sausage rolls, but these moreish filo cigars are a world apart. Filled with shredded spiced lamb with a hint of chilli and plenty of herbs, they're simply begging to be dunked into a yoghurt dip freshened up with cucumber and sumac. Don't be put off by the long cooking time – you can slow-cook and shred the lamb the day before, then assemble and bake the cigars on the day you plan to serve.

Makes 12
Cooking time: 5 hours
plus overnight marinating time and cooling time

Lamb cigars

800g of lamb shoulder, bone in

½ tsp ground cumin

½ tsp ground coriander

¼ tsp sea salt

¼ tsp freshly ground black pepper

½ onion, roughly chopped

1 carrot, roughly chopped

1 red chilli, roughly chopped

150ml of water

1 tsp mint jelly

1 handful of coriander leaves, chopped

1 handful of parsley leaves, chopped

½ tsp sumac

4 sheets of filo pastry

40g of unsalted butter, melted

Cumin seeds, for sprinkling

Dip

120g of natural yoghurt

½ cucumber, deseeded

1 handful of mint leaves, finely chopped

½ tsp sumac

Mix together the cumin, coriander, salt and pepper and rub all over the lamb. Leave to marinate overnight in the fridge.

The next day, Preheat an oven to 160°C. Place the lamb in a snugly fitting casserole dish with the onion, carrot, chilli and water. Cover with a lid or foil and cook for 3½-4 hours, until falling apart.

Carefully lift out the lamb and set aside, then strain the braising liquid through a fine sieve into a clean pan. Skim off as much fat as you can, then place over a medium heat and leave to reduce by about a third. Meanwhile, remove the bone from the shoulder and roughly chop the meat against the grain. Transfer to a bowl and stir through the mint jelly, herbs and sumac. Add the reduced braising liquid a little at a time until you have a mixture that clings together (you may not need all the liquid). Allow to cool completely, then divide into 12 equal portions.

To make the cigars, preheat an oven to 160°C. Work with only 1 sheet of filo at a time to prevent them from drying out. Cut the sheet into 3 rectangles roughly measuring 12x20cm, then spoon a portion of the lamb onto the bottom third of each rectangle. Brush the pastry around it with the melted butter, then fold in the sides and start rolling the pastry up around the lamb into a cigar shape. Continue rolling until all the pastry is wrapped around the meat, then place on a tray lined with baking paper. Repeat until all the pastry and lamb is used up.

Brush the tops of each cigar with more melted butter, then sprinkle over some cumin seeds. Bake in the oven for 20 minutes, or until crisp and dark brown around the edges.

While the cigars bake, coarsely grate the cucumber. Squeeze the cucumber in a j-cloth to remove excess water, then stir into the yoghurt with the mint, sumac and a pinch of salt. Serve alongside the cigars.

Crostini with broad bean pesto, fresh cheese and oven-dried tomatoes

Crostini are the ultimate little snack to enjoy with drinks – this recipe allows you to show off your culinary credentials with some homemade ricotta and a fresh, sprightly broad bean pesto. If you're short on time you can simply use shop-bought ricotta, but it's well worth making yourself as it's such an easy, rewarding thing to create in the kitchen.

Makes 12 crostini
Cooking time: 1 hour
plus 2 extra hours if making the cheese

Homemade ricotta

500ml of organic whole milk

1 lemon, juiced and zested

Tomatoes

6 cherry tomatoes

1 sprig of rosemary, leaves picked and finely chopped

½ garlic clove, finely chopped

1 tbsp olive oil

Broad bean pesto

250g of broad beans, fresh or frozen (podded weight)

½ garlic clove

15g of Parmesan, or a vegetarian Italian hard cheese, grated

5 mint leaves, or basil leaves

30ml of extra virgin olive oil

1 lemon, juiced

Crostini

1 small baguette

Olive oil, for brushing

Begin by making the ricotta. Pour the milk into a saucepan and heat until it is just below boiling point. Remove from the heat then stir in the lemon juice to split the milk. Set aside for 10 minutes. Meanwhile, set up a large sieve over a bowl and line the sieve with a j-cloth. Pour the contents of the pan into the j-cloth, then leave to strain in the fridge for 1 hour. Give the mixture a stir every now and then to help remove the remaining liquid.

After an hour, you should be left with some solid curds in the j-cloth, with all the liquid whey in the bowl. You don't need the whey for this recipe but it is a fantastic ingredient to use in baking or as a marinade to tenderise meat. Transfer the curds into a bowl and mix in the lemon zest and plenty of salt and pepper. Reserve in the fridge.

Preheat an oven to 150°C. Halve the cherry tomatoes and place them cut-side up on a tray. Mix the rosemary and garlic into the oil with a pinch of salt and pepper, then use this to coat the tomatoes. Roast the tomatoes for 45 minutes, until just starting to wrinkle and dry out.

Meanwhile, make the pesto. Defrost the beans if they're frozen, then peel the paler shell off each bean by gently squeezing them at the base – the brighter green bean within should pop out. This is a little time-consuming, but the outer shells can be slightly bitter so your pesto will be much nicer as a result.

Recipe continues overleaf

Recipe continued

Crush the garlic to a paste with a pinch of salt in a pestle and mortar, then add the Parmesan and mint (or basil) leaves and grind to a thick paste. Add the beans a few at a time and smash them into a coarse pesto, then mix in the oil and season to taste with salt, pepper and lemon juice.

Preheat an oven to 200°C. Slice the baguette at an angle into 12 thin 1cm slices, then arrange on a baking tray. Brush with a little oil, season with salt and pepper then bake for 8-10 minutes until golden and crisp, turning the crostini halfway through so they're cooked evenly.

When ready to serve, spread some ricotta on each piece of toast and top with a spoonful of the pesto. Finish with a halved tomato and eat immediately.

Leek kebabs with pickled mussels
by Sam Buckley

Pickled cockles used to be offered in pubs across the country with a pint or two for good reason – the briny, tangy flavour worked wonders with the malty sweetness of ale. Chef Sam Buckley brings the idea into the twenty-first century with these incredible pickled mussels, served alongside barbecued leek kebabs and a sauce made from the green tops. Enjoy in the sun with your favourite beer.

Serves 6
Cooking time: 1 hour 30 minutes
Equipment: 6 metal skewers, blender

Leeks

6 leeks, washed

1l of water

50g of sea salt, plus extra for seasoning

100g of stock – any kind works but make sure it's good quality

Rapeseed oil, for brushing

Apple cider vinegar, to taste

Mussels

6 handfuls of mussels – Sam uses Shetland mussels

1 dash of rapeseed oil

100ml of water

2 tbsp capers, drained, to serve

Pickle liquor

100ml of apple cider vinegar

50g of caster sugar

150ml of water

Cut the leeks in half where the white meets the green. Cut the white parts in half lengthways, then into thumb-sized pieces, taking care so they don't fall apart. Stack these pieces onto 6 metal skewers so they sit horizontally on top of one another.

Pour a litre of water into a bowl and stir in the salt. Submerge the kebabs in this brine for 1 hour – this tenderises and thoroughly seasons the leeks.

Meanwhile, clean the mussels by pulling off any stringy fibres from the shells and giving them a good rinse under running water. Discard any that don't close when firmly tapped.

Place a lidded frying pan over a high heat and wait until it's smoking hot. Add a dash of oil then tip in the mussels along with the water and cover. Cook for 5 minutes, or as soon as the mussels begin to open. Discard any mussels which don't open when tapped. Drain the mussels, reserving the cooking liquor, then when cool enough to handle pick the meat from the shells and reserve in the fridge.

Bring a pan of water to the boil. Finely slice the green parts of the leeks, give them a good wash, then boil for 1 minute. They will still be bright green but should give with a little pressure between your thumb and forefinger. Place them into iced water to chill and reserve their colour, then drain thoroughly by squeezing them in a tea towel. Reserve 100ml of the water used to cook them.

Recipe continues overleaf

Recipe continued

Place the green leeks in a blender with the stock and the reserved leek cooking water. Strain the reserved mussel cooking liquor through a fine sieve into the blender, leaving a little behind which may contain some grit and sand. Blitz until bright green and smooth, then season to taste with salt and apple cider vinegar.

To pickle the mussels, make a pickling liquor. Place the vinegar, caster sugar and 150ml of water into a pan and heat until the sugar dissolves. Place in the fridge to chill. Half an hour before you plan to serve, submerge the picked mussels in the chilled liquor to pickle.

When ready to serve, light a barbecue or place a griddle pan over a very high heat. Pull the leek skewers out of the brine and pat them dry, then brush with a little rapeseed oil. Place on the grill or in the pan and cook until charred evenly all over, turning regularly. Meanwhile, very gently heat the green sauce.

To serve, spoon the sauce onto a serving platter or into individual bowls and place the charred leek skewers on top. Drain the pickled mussels and arrange alongside, then serve with a final drizzle of oil and the capers on the side for people to add as they like at the table.

Caponata
by Matt Beardmore

The description of Caponata – a Sicilian aubergine stew – doesn't really do the dish justice. It's an incredible celebration of the island's sunshine flavours, with pine nuts, raisins and capers adding little bursts of flavour and texture throughout. It's best served at room temperature, so benefits from being made in advance.

Serves 4-6
Cooking time: 1 hour 45 minutes

4 aubergines
100ml of extra virgin olive oil
4 garlic cloves, finely sliced
1 tin (400g) of tinned plum tomatoes
4 celery sticks, finely sliced
500ml of vegetable oil, for deep-frying
2 white onions, finely chopped
100g of pitted Kalamata olives
1½ tbsp pine nuts
1½ tbsp raisins
1 tbsp capers, drained
2 tsp caster sugar
60ml of red wine vinegar
½ bunch of basil, leaves picked
½ bunch of mint, leaves picked

Cut the aubergines into 3cm cubes, place them into a large colander and sprinkle generously with salt, tossing to combine. Leave to drain for 1 hour.

Place a small saucepan over a low heat and add around 40ml of the olive oil. Gently sauté the garlic for a few minutes until very soft but not brown, then strain the juice from the tinned tomatoes and add them in, crushing them with the back of a spoon. Turn up the heat slightly and leave to cook for 30 minutes, stirring occasionally, until you have a rich sauce and the oil rises to the surface. If the sauce is ready before you complete the other elements, turn the heat down to its lowest setting and keep warm.

Meanwhile, bring a pan of salted water to the boil. Add the celery and boil for a few minutes, until cooked but still retaining a slight bite. Drain and set aside.

Pour the vegetable oil into a saucepan and heat to 180°C. Working in batches, deep-fry the aubergines for 5 minutes, or until soft and golden. Drain on kitchen paper and set aside.

Place a large saucepan over a medium-low heat and add the remaining olive oil. Add the onions and cook for 5 minutes, until soft and translucent. Add the olives, pine nuts, raisins, capers and cooked celery and cook for a further minute, then pour in the tomato sauce. Cook for 2-3 minutes.

Remove the pan from the heat and fold in the aubergines. Dissolve the sugar in the vinegar and stir it into the caponata, tasting as you go – add a little more sugar if needed. Season with salt to taste and allow to cool to room temperature. At this stage you can store the caponata in the fridge overnight, but ensure it is back up to room temperature before serving.

When ready to serve, gently tear in the basil and mint leaves and transfer to a serving dish.

Barbecued beef pavé with yeast butter, cumin carrots and nasturtium salad
by Adam Bennett

Pavé is a special cut of beef – taken from the heart of the rump or sirloin it contains no fat or connective tissue; much like the more expensive fillet but with bags more flavour. Chef Adam Bennett barbecues the steak and dresses it in plenty of savoury yeast butter, with cumin and lemon-dressed charred carrots and a garden nasturtium salad on the side. Any leftover butter freezes well and is great melted over vegetables.

Serves 4
Cooking time: 1 hour

1 pavé of beef, weighing approx. 500g, cut from the rump end of the sirloin – Adam suggests Irish Hereford beef

16 medium carrots, ideally new season, with their tops

Olive oil, for brushing

1 handful of nasturtium leaves, with a few flowers if available

Yeast butter

100g of salted butter, softened

½ tbsp yeast flakes

½ tsp freshly ground black pepper

½ tbsp chives, finely chopped

½ tbsp parsley, finely chopped

Dressing

3 tsp cumin seeds

30g of preserved lemon, drained and finely diced

100g of extra virgin olive oil

5g of garlic, finely chopped

1 pinch of Korean red pepper powder (gochugaru), or medium chilli flakes

1 pinch of caster sugar

Begin by making the butter. Add 30g of the butter to a small frying pan over a medium heat – once it begins to foam, add the yeast flakes. Cook, stirring constantly, until the yeast start to turn golden. Pour into a bowl and allow to cool, then mix with the remaining butter, pepper and herbs. Set aside.

To make the dressing, toast the cumin seeds in a hot, dry frying pan for 30 seconds or until fragrant, then tip them into a pestle and mortar. Leave to cool, then crush to a coarse powder. Combine the ground cumin seeds with the preserved lemon, olive oil and garlic, then add the chilli flakes and caster sugar to taste (you may not need all of the sugar and chilli). Set aside.

Light a barbecue well in advance to allow the coals to come to temperature. Bring the beef out of the fridge at least 30 minutes before you cook it. Finely chop the carrot tops then wash the carrots well. Lightly coat them in oil and a little salt.

When ready to cook, season the beef generously with salt and pepper, then place it on the grill with the carrots alongside. After 1 minute, flip the beef, then continue flipping it regularly until it is cooked to your liking (around 8 minutes for medium-rare). Turn the carrots as they cook too, until just beginning to char. The beef will finish cooking before the carrots, so once it's done leave it to rest for 15 minutes.

When the carrots have finished cooking, remove them from the barbecue. Stir a handful of the carrot tops into the dressing, then toss in the carrots. Place the nasturtium leaves and flowers in a bowl and add a little of the cumin dressing, tossing to combine.

Give the beef a final coating of yeast butter, then carve against the grain into slices and season with salt. Arrange the slices on a serving platter with the carrots and nasturtium salad. Serve with extra yeast butter on the side.

One Pots

Tuscan seafood stew

What was once a humble dish enjoyed by Italian fishermen is now the pinnacle of luxury, thanks to the melange of different fish and seafood in this incredible stew. With a rich red wine base full of slowly simmered octopus and squid, this is a showstopping pot to bring to the table – feel free to chop and change the fish you use to whatever's at its best.

Serves 6
Cooking time: 2 hours

Stew base

3 tbsp olive oil

1 tsp chilli flakes

1 tsp fennel seeds

1 onion, finely chopped

4 garlic cloves, finely chopped

1 celery stick, finely chopped

1 small octopus, weighing approx. 500g, cleaned and sliced

1 small squid, cleaned and sliced into rings

2 sprigs of sage

250ml of red wine

400ml of passata

1l of fish stock

Fish and seafood

200g of monkfish tail, cut into 6 pieces

200g of gurnard fillet, cut into 6 pieces

200g of red snapper fillet, cut into 6 pieces

6 langoustines

200g of clams, cleaned

200g of mussels, cleaned

To finish

6 slices of good bread

2 garlic cloves, peeled

1 handful of flat-leaf parsley, chopped

Set a large lidded casserole dish over a medium heat and add 2 tablespoons of the olive oil, the chilli flakes and fennel seeds. Once aromatic, add the onion, garlic and celery with a pinch of salt and cook for around 10 minutes, until the onions are soft but without colour.

Remove the vegetables from the pan with a slotted spoon and set aside. Turn up the heat to high, add the remaining tablespoon of oil and then the octopus and squid. Cook, stirring regularly, for 15 minutes, or until the liquid released from the octopus has evaporated.

Add the vegetables back to the pan along with the sage and red wine. Bring to a simmer and reduce by half, then add the passata and 600ml of the fish stock. Cook for 1 hour, stirring occasionally, until the octopus is tender and the sauce is thick.

Add the remaining fish stock, then nestle the pieces of monkfish, gurnard and red snapper into the stew. Place the langoustines on top, cover with a lid and simmer for 5 minutes. Lift the lid off, tip in the clams and mussels (discarding any which don't close when tapped firmly on a hard surface), then cover and cook for a final 3-4 minutes, until the shells have opened up.

Discard any mussels or clams which haven't opened, then turn off the heat and leave the stew to rest for a few minutes while you toast the bread. Rub the garlic cloves over the toast. To serve, scatter the parsley over the stew and bring to the table with the toast to help mop up all that rich red sauce.

Venison cobbler with cheddar and rosemary scones

An all-in-one dish full of hearty, autumnal flavour, cobbler ensures everyone gets a hefty helping of rich venison stew and a few buttery, cheesy scones to soak up the sauce. Be patient when reducing the port and red wine – they're key to giving the cobbler its background sweetness and body.

Serves 6
Cooking time: 2 hours
Equipment: Food processor, 7cm round cutter

Cobbler

Rapeseed oil, for frying

1 onion, diced

4 garlic cloves, finely sliced

2 celery sticks, sliced

2 carrots, peeled and roughly chopped

200g of smoked pancetta

1kg of diced venison

2 tbsp of plain flour

200g of button mushrooms, halved

6 juniper berries, crushed

2 sprigs of fresh thyme

1 sprig of rosemary

2 bay leaves

200ml of port

300ml of red wine

300ml of beef stock

1 tbsp redcurrant jelly

1 orange, zested

Scones

450g of self-raising flour, plus extra for dusting

1 tbsp of baking powder

120g of unsalted butter

2 tbsp of rosemary leaves, finely chopped

150g of mature cheddar, finely grated

350ml of whole milk

1 egg, beaten

Place a large casserole dish over a medium heat and add a splash of oil. Once hot, add the onion, garlic, celery, carrot, pancetta and a pinch of salt and cook for 10 minutes until softened, then use a slotted spoon to transfer to a plate. Turn the heat up under the dish and add another splash of oil.

Dust the venison in flour and season well with salt and pepper. Working in batches, brown the venison all over in the casserole dish, transferring each batch to the bowl with the softened vegetables as you work. When all the venison is browned, tip the vegetables and meat back into the dish, along with the mushrooms, juniper berries, herbs and port. Bring to a simmer, then continue to cook until the port has reduced by half. Add the wine, then allow to reduce by half again. Pour in the beef stock with the redcurrant jelly and orange zest, then leave to simmer uncovered for 1 hour, stirring occasionally.

Meanwhile, make the scones. Place the flour, baking powder, a pinch of salt and the butter in a food processor and pulse until it has the consistency of wet sand. Add the rosemary and three-quarters of the cheese, pulse again until just combined, then start adding the milk bit by bit, pulsing as you go, until a dough starts to clump together (you may not need to use all the milk). Bring the dough together into a ball. Place into a bowl, cover and leave to rest for 20 minutes in the fridge. Preheat an oven to 170°C.

Once rested, tip the dough out onto a lightly floured work surface and roll out until around 3.5cm thick. Use a 7cm round cutter to stamp out the scones. Brush the tops of each scone with beaten egg then sprinkle over the remaining cheese.

Place the scones on top of the stew (any extra scones can be placed on a separate tray) and transfer to the oven. You may want to place a tray underneath as the stew might bubble up over the sides during cooking. Cook for 30-40 minutes, or until the scones are golden on top.

Roast chicken Marbella

Chicken Marbella is one of those fantastic retro dishes that doesn't get the attention it deserves these days. Here, its flavours are imbued with a rice-stuffed chicken, full of sweet prunes, briny olives and plenty of white wine and sherry. A guaranteed crowd-pleaser that offers something different for a Sunday roast; serve it alongside buttered greens and bread to feed a particularly hungry crowd.

Serves 4-6
Cooking time: 2 hours 30 minutes

Chicken

1 large free-range chicken, weighing approx. 1.6kg

1 tbsp olive oil

1 tsp dried thyme

1 tsp dried oregano

Stuffing

1 garlic bulb

Olive oil, for frying

40g of unsalted butter

1 onion, finely chopped

100g of brown basmati rice

600ml of chicken stock

80g of prunes, pitted and halved

6 sprigs of oregano, leaves picked

¼ bunch of parsley, leaves picked

1 lemon, zested

1 tsp sherry vinegar

Marbella sauce

100ml of dry sherry

300ml of white wine

60g of caperberries, or 2 tbsp capers, drained

100g of green olives stuffed with anchovies, or 100g of pitted green olives plus 5 anchovy fillets, roughly chopped

4 banana shallots, peeled and halved lengthways (keep the root attached so the layers stay together)

Preheat an oven to 200°C. For the stuffing, slice the top off the garlic bulb to reveal the cloves, then place on a square of foil. Drizzle with a little olive oil and wrap tightly. Roast in the oven for 30 minutes.

Meanwhile, add a splash of oil and the butter to a saucepan. Add the onion and cook for 15 minutes, until caramelised and soft. Wash the rice, then tip into the pan and toast for a few minutes. Add the chicken stock and simmer for 25 minutes, until the rice is just cooked.

After the garlic is cooked, remove from the oven and turn the heat down to 180°C. Squeeze the cloves from their skins and stir through the brown rice. Mix in the prunes, herbs, lemon zest and sherry vinegar. Season to taste with salt and pepper.

Spoon the stuffing into the chicken, then drizzle with oil and sprinkle over the herbs with plenty of salt and pepper. Take a large, deep roasting tray and pour in the dry sherry and white wine, along with the caperberries, olives and shallots. Sit the chicken on top, then cook in the oven for 1½ hours. If the chicken browns too quickly after 1 hour, cover it with foil.

Check the chicken is cooked by inserting a skewer into the thickest part of the thigh – the juices should run clear. Leave to rest for 15-20 minutes, then divide the stuffing between plates, carve the chicken and make sure everyone gets a good amount of the cooking juices, olives, shallots and capers poured over their dish.

Duck leg tagine

Slow-cooked duck legs are shredded and stirred through this rich stew, flavoured with Moroccan spices and sweetened with tomatoes and prunes. A stunning dish which warms and awakens the senses in an instant. Replace the couscous with rice or breads depending on what you're in the mood for. It also tastes even better if cooked the day before and reheated, so it's great to prepare in advance when entertaining.

Serves 6
Cooking time: 3 hours 20 minutes

Tagine

Olive oil, for frying

3 red onions, finely sliced

5 garlic cloves, finely sliced

4 tbsp ras el hanout

2 pinches of saffron

2 tsp ground ginger

2 cinnamon sticks

2 tbsp harissa

4 large duck legs

2 tins (800g) of chopped tomatoes

1l of chicken stock

2 preserved lemons, drained

2 Maris Piper potatoes, peeled and chopped into 2cm chunks

200g of prunes, pitted and halved

100g of pitted Kalamata olives

Couscous

600ml of chicken stock

300g of couscous

2 handfuls of sultanas

¼ bunch of coriander, chopped

¼ bunch of mint, leaves picked and chopped

To serve

¼ bunch of coriander, chopped

¼ bunch of parsley, chopped

40g of flaked almonds, toasted

Heat a splash of oil in a tagine or heavy-bottomed saucepan and add the onions, garlic and a pinch of salt. Cook for 5 minutes or until just starting to soften, then add the ras el hanout, saffron, ginger, cinnamon sticks and harissa. Stir and cook for another minute, then add the duck legs, tinned tomatoes and cover with chicken stock.

Quarter the preserved lemons and scrape out the flesh, discarding any seeds. Add half the flesh to the pan (discarding the other half), then finely chop the peel and add it to the pan too. Bring to a simmer, then cover and turn the heat down to low. Cook for 2 hours.

After 2 hours, carefully lift the duck legs out of the pan and use a fork to strip the meat from the bones. Discard the bones and skin, then return the meat to the pan along with the potatoes, prunes and olives. Cook uncovered, stirring occasionally, for 1 hour, or until the potatoes are soft. You may need to add a splash of water every so often if the tagine begins sticking to the bottom of the pan.

Once the potatoes are tender, turn off the heat, season to taste with salt and pepper and set aside to rest while you prepare the couscous. Bring the chicken stock to the boil and place the couscous in a lidded heatproof container. Pour over the boiling stock, cover and leave to stand for 10 minutes.

To serve, fluff up the couscous with a fork and transfer to a serving bowl, stirring in the sultanas and herbs, then season to taste with salt and pepper. Sprinkle the tagine with the coriander, parsley and flaked almonds.

Sausage and fennel lasagne with chilli garlic bread

Of all the dishes in the world, few bring a family together quite like a lasagne. This recipe takes inspiration from Sicily, where the combination of pork and fennel is king. You can make both the ragù and bechamel sauce a day in advance if needed.

Serves 6
Cooking time: 2 hours 45 minutes

Ragù

3 tbsp olive oil

1 tbsp fennel seeds

1 tsp chilli flakes

1 onion, finely chopped

3 garlic cloves, finely sliced

½ fennel bulb, finely diced

10 pork and fennel sausages

250ml of white wine

2 tins (800g) of chopped tomatoes

1 bay leaf

Bechamel

75g of unsalted butter

75g of plain flour

2 bay leaves

900ml of whole milk, warmed

Freshly grated nutmeg, to taste

1 dash of white wine vinegar

Pasta

6 fresh lasagne sheets

20g of Parmesan, finely grated

Chilli garlic bread

80g of unsalted butter, softened

1 red chilli, finely chopped

2 large garlic cloves, finely grated

2 sprigs of basil, leaves picked and finely chopped

1 large ciabatta

Pour the olive oil into a large saucepan over a medium-low heat. Add the fennel seeds and chilli flakes, leave to sizzle for 1 minute, then tip in the onion, garlic and fennel. Cook, stirring regularly, for 15 minutes until soft. Lift them out and set aside.

Split the sausages and discard the skins, then add the sausage meat into the same pan. Break down the meat using the back of a wooden spoon and cook for 8-10 minutes, until well browned and caramelised all over. Return the vegetables to the pan, pour in the white wine to deglaze and scrape the bottom of the pan with your spoon. Simmer until the wine has reduced by half. Add the tomatoes, bay leaf and a pinch of salt and pepper, then leave to gently cook over a low heat for 1 hour.

Meanwhile, make the bechamel. Melt the butter in a pan then add the flour. Cook for a few minutes, whisking constantly, then add the bay leaves. Gradually whisk in the milk, then cook over a low heat for 8 minutes, whisking constantly. Grate in a little nutmeg, add the vinegar and season with salt and pepper. Remove from the heat and cover with a sheet of cling film.

Preheat an oven to 180°C. Take a large baking dish – approximately 30x20cm in size – and add a layer of ragù across the base. Top with lasagne sheets, then spread over a layer of bechamel. Repeat until everything is used up, but make sure the final layer is pasta topped with bechamel. Sprinkle over the grated Parmesan then bake in the oven for 45 minutes.

While the lasagne cooks, make the garlic bread. Place the softened butter in a bowl and mix in the chilli, garlic, basil and a pinch of salt and pepper. Cut 12 slits into the ciabatta, ensuring you don't slice all the way through the loaf, then carefully spread the butter inside each slit.

When the lasagne is ready, remove from the oven and leave to rest. Meanwhile, place the garlic bread into the oven and cook for 10-15 minutes. Bring both to the table and dig in.

Mushroom ragù with pappardelle and crispy garlic breadcrumbs

When cooking vegan dishes, mushrooms are a sure-fire way of generating plenty of depth and umami-rich 'meatiness'. This ragù replaces mince with blitzed chestnut mushrooms which are patiently caramelised until crisp and brown. With larger, juicier pieces of shiitake and portobello strewn throughout and a touch of crunch added thanks to some herby garlic breadcrumbs, this is a warming bowlful of flavour.

Serves 6
Cooking time: 2 hours 15 minutes
Equipment: Food processor

Ragù

800g of chestnut mushrooms

3 tbsp extra virgin olive oil

4 garlic cloves, finely chopped

2 celery sticks, finely sliced

2 carrots, finely diced

1 large onion, finely chopped

2 tbsp soy sauce

200ml of red wine

3 tins (1.2kg) of chopped tomatoes

2 tbsp tomato purée

2 tsp sugar

4 sprigs of thyme

2 bay leaves

200g of shiitake mushrooms

3 portobello mushrooms, roughly chopped

350g of dried pappardelle

Breadcrumbs

2 tbsp extra virgin olive oil

50g of panko breadcrumbs

2 garlic cloves, finely grated

1 lemon, zested

1 handful of parsley leaves, finely chopped

Working in batches, blitz the chestnut mushrooms in a food processor until they resemble mince. In a large saucepan, heat the olive oil and add the garlic, celery, carrot and onion. Cook for 15 minutes over a medium-low heat until soft but not coloured. Add the mushroom 'mince' and soy sauce, then turn the heat up to high. Cook, stirring regularly, for 30 minutes, until all the liquid released from the mushrooms has evaporated and they have started to caramelise – be patient!

Add the wine to deglaze, scraping the bottom of the pan as you do so, then simmer for another 10 minutes until almost dry again. Pour in the tomatoes along with the tomato purée, sugar, thyme, bay leaves and a pinch of salt and pepper. Add the shiitake and portobello mushrooms, then simmer gently with the lid on for 30 minutes.

Meanwhile, fry the panko breadcrumbs in the extra virgin olive oil until just beginning to colour, then add in the grated garlic. Cook for another minute until the breadcrumbs are crisp, then drain the mixture on kitchen paper. Transfer to a bowl and stir in the lemon zest and parsley with a pinch of salt.

After 30 minutes, remove the lid and continue cooking the mushroom ragù until thickened (around another 30 minutes). When the ragù is ready, turn the heat down to its lowest setting and bring a large pan of salted water to the boil.

Cook the pappardelle for 8-10 minutes (depending on whether you like it al dente or not) then drain, reserving a cup of the pasta water. Stir the pasta into the ragù, adding a splash of pasta water to loosen and help everything come together, then divide between bowls. Serve immediately with the breadcrumbs sprinkled on top.

Pork shoulder with braised fennel and pinto beans

A mammoth tower of pork shoulder sits on a bed of braised beans and fennel in this rustic sharing dish ideal for getting the family around the table. The stew absorbs all the richness of the pork as they slowly cook together in the oven and the shatteringly crunchy crackling finishes things off delectably.

Serves 6
Cooking time: 3 hours 30 minutes
plus overnight soaking and
marinating time

Pork

1 pork shoulder

½ tsp black peppercorns

1 tsp fennel seeds

1 tsp coriander seeds

2 garlic cloves, roughly chopped

1 lemon, zested

1 tsp sea salt

Stew

180g of dried pinto beans

3 tbsp extra virgin olive oil, plus extra for finishing

1 tsp fennel seeds

½ tsp coriander seeds

1 banana shallot, sliced

1 leek, white part only, sliced

3 large garlic cloves, finely sliced

1 large fennel bulb, fronds removed and cut into 6-8 wedges

1 tsp sea salt

400ml of white wine

2 sprigs of thyme

2 sprigs of sage

1 lemon, zested

500ml of chicken stock

The day before you plan to serve, cover the pinto beans with cold water and leave to soak overnight. Cut away the skin from the pork shoulder and set aside. Trim off any thick areas of fat (this ensures the stew doesn't become greasy).

Toast the peppercorns, fennel seeds and coriander seeds in a dry frying pan for 30 seconds, or until fragrant, then grind in a pestle and mortar with the garlic, lemon zest and salt. Rub this mixture all over the pork shoulder. Score the reserved skin in 1cm intervals, then place back on top of the pork and secure in place with a skewer or toothpicks. Place in the fridge to marinate overnight – leaving it uncovered will help to dry out the skin and ensure extra-crisp crackling.

The next day, take the pork out of the fridge to allow to come to room temperature before cooking. To make the stew, heat the olive oil in a large casserole dish and add the fennel seeds and coriander seeds. Once they begin to crackle, add the shallot, leek, garlic, fennel and salt. Cook for 8 minutes, or until the vegetables are soft and have started to caramelise slightly, then tip in the drained beans, white wine, herbs and lemon zest. Push the stew to the sides of the dish and place the pork in the centre, then continue to cook on the hob until the wine has almost reduced completely (around 10 minutes). Meanwhile, preheat an oven to 170°C.

Add some of the stock to the dish then transfer to the oven and cook for 2½ hours, topping up occasionally with more stock as needed. When the beans are tender and the skin on top of the pork has turned into crackling, remove from the oven and leave to rest for 10-15 minutes.

To serve, bring the dish to the table, break the crackling into shards and carve the pork into thick slices. Dish out the stew and top with the pork and crackling.

Artichoke risotto
by Charlie Hibbert

When done right risotto is a wondrous dish, offering all the silky richness you could ever ask for. Charlie Hibbert's recipe is a classic and includes the fabulously sweet and mildly nutty flavour of fresh artichokes, a fantastic vegetable that's rarely used in home kitchens.

Serves 6
Cooking time: 1 hour

Artichokes

15 violet artichokes

1 lemon

Risotto

1.5l of chicken or vegetable stock, preferably homemade

1 large onion

1 celery heart (the pale leafy centre from a bunch of celery)

100g of unsalted butter

1 squeeze of lemon juice

400g of risotto rice, either Vialone, Carnaroli or Arborio varieties

125ml of dry white wine

120g of Parmesan

Begin by preparing the artichokes. Squeeze the lemon juice into a large bowl of water. Snap off the outer leaves of the artichoke, then begin trimming away any dark green flesh from around the base, leaving you with the pale yellow heart at the centre. Cut off any remaining leaves, then give the stem part a quick trim with a knife. Place the artichoke into the lemon water as soon as you're done to prevent it browning, then repeat with the remaining artichokes.

Pour the stock into a large saucepan and bring to a simmer. Meanwhile, finely chop the onion and finely slice the celery heart. Add half the butter to a wide, shallow pan over a medium heat. Once melted, add the onion and celery and cover. Cook for 3-4 minutes until softened, then add a squeeze of lemon juice and season with a pinch of salt and pepper. Add the rice, stir for a minute to coat it in the butter, then pour in the wine and simmer, uncovered, until it has almost all been absorbed by the rice.

Add a ladleful of the simmering stock to the rice, then stir continuously until the rice absorbs all the stock. Repeat this process, adding a ladleful of stock and then stirring until absorbed, until the rice is tender throughout without any bite to it. You may not need to use all the stock, so after around half of it has been absorbed start tasting the rice until you're happy with the texture.

After around 10 minutes of adding the stock, slice the artichokes into ½cm-thick discs. Stir them into the risotto – they will gently cook through with the rice.

Once you're happy with the texture of the rice, remove the risotto from the heat and allow to rest for 3 minutes. Meanwhile, finely grate the Parmesan. Vigorously beat in the grated Parmesan and the remaining 50g of butter, then season to taste with salt and pepper. Divide between serving bowls and serve.

Mutton chop hotpot
by Stosie Madi

Neck chops are incredibly flavoursome as they contain more fat than regular chops from the loin. If you can get them, mutton chops are the most flavourful of all. This dish takes the traditional Lancashire hotpot to the next level, with proud French-trimmed bones breaking through the golden buttery potato crust. If you're struggling to find mutton chops then lamb is delicious too; you can also use regular cutlets.

Serves 4
Cooking time: 2 hours 15 minutes
plus overnight marinating time
Equipment: Blender

Chops

12 mutton (or lamb) neck chops, or cutlets, French-trimmed

50ml of vegetable oil

1 tbsp cumin seeds, toasted and ground

1 tbsp thyme leaves, chopped

2 tbsp rosemary leaves, chopped

1 tbsp fennel, chopped

1 tin of anchovy fillets in oil

2 garlic cloves, chopped

30g of unsalted butter

Filling

2 large turnips, peeled and roughly diced

75g of unsalted butter, softened

150g of peas, freshly podded if in season (frozen if not)

150g of green beans

3 banana shallots, finely sliced

30ml of white wine vinegar

500ml of lamb stock

350g of Maris Piper potatoes

2 tbsp cumin seeds, toasted

1 bunch of rosemary, leaves picked and finely chopped

Begin by marinating the mutton (or lamb). Trim off the outer fat of the chops and reserve. Place the oil, cumin, herbs, fennel, anchovies and garlic in a blender and blitz into a paste. Season the chops well with salt and pepper, then rub the marinade into the meat, keeping the bones as clean as possible. Cover and leave in the fridge overnight.

Take the trimmed fat and place in a cold pan. Gently heat, rendering as much fat as possible, then weigh out 30g of the melted fat (discarding any solids). Mix this with the butter, then reserve in the fridge.

The next day, preheat an oven to 200°C. Toss the diced turnips in a roasting tray with 50g of the butter and a pinch of salt. Roast until tender – the timing will depend on the turnips, but check them after 30 minutes. Meanwhile, sweat down the shallots in the remaining 25g of butter and a pinch of salt until soft and just beginning to colour. Once both are cooked, leave to cool.

Arrange the marinated chops in a deep earthenware or ovenproof casserole dish, so that the bones overlap with the meat in the centre. Sprinkle the peas and beans into the dish, then the shallots and finally the turnips. Season with salt and pepper then sprinkle the vinegar over everything. Pour in the lamb stock until everything is covered (you may not need it all).

Preheat the oven to 150°C. Peel the potatoes then slice as finely as possible, using a mandoline if you have one. Gently melt the rendered fat and butter mixture, then start layering the sliced potatoes on top of the dish, brushing them liberally with the butter mixture and sprinkling each layer with a little salt, some cumin seeds and rosemary. Transfer the dish to the oven and cook for 1 hour, until the potatoes are soft, then turn up the temperature to 180°C and cook for a further 10 minutes, or until the potatoes are crisp. Serve immediately.

Tariwala murgh (Punjabi chicken curry)
by Rohit Ghai

A comforting, balanced, deliciously moreish dish that reminds us all why Britain is head-over-heels in love with Indian food, Rohit Ghai's 'home-style' chicken curry is simply a joy to eat. Best of all, it's ready in under an hour and is guaranteed to be a hit with everyone around the table.

Serves 4-6
Cooking time: 40 minutes

75ml of rapeseed oil, or mustard oil

1 cinnamon stick

2 black cardamom pods

4 cloves

2 dried bay leaves

1 tsp coriander seeds, crushed

250g of onion, finely chopped

1 tbsp ginger paste

1 tbsp garlic paste

½ tsp red chilli powder

¼ tsp turmeric powder

1 tbsp ground coriander

1 tsp garam masala

100g of chopped tomatoes, or tomato purée

12 boneless chicken thighs, or drumsticks (or a mix of both)

50g of plain yoghurt

2 tbsp coriander leaves, chopped, to garnish

Cooked rice, or roti, to serve

Pour the oil into a heavy-bottomed saucepan over a medium heat. Add the cinnamon stick, cardamom pods, cloves, bay leaves and coriander seeds – as soon as they begin to sizzle and crackle, add the onion and fry for 5-7 minutes, or until softened and beginning to turn golden.

Add the ginger and garlic pastes, cook for a further few minutes until fragrant, then add the chilli powder, turmeric, ground coriander, garam masala and chopped tomatoes (or purée). Fry for a few minutes, stirring regularly, adding a splash of water if the mixture catches on the bottom of the pan.

When you start to see the oil being released around the sides of the pan, add the chicken and mix well. Turn down the heat to low, cover and cook for 4 minutes.

Beat the yoghurt to ensure it is nice and smooth, then mix it into the curry. If the pan is looking quite dry or you prefer a curry with more sauce, add a splash of water. Cover the pan again and turn the temperature up slightly, then leave to cook for 10-12 minutes, or until the chicken is completely cooked through. Season to taste with salt. At this point, you can pick out and discard the whole spices if preferred.

To serve, garnish the curry with coriander leaves and bring to the table with rice or breads.

Dinner Party Starters

Juniper beef carpaccio with pickled shallots, pear and Parmesan mayo

Fine slices of juniper-flavoured beef fillet are layered up with piquant pickled shallots, pear, walnuts and a homemade Parmesan mayonnaise to create an incredible starter that looks seriously cheffy. All the elements can be prepared in advance – if you're freezing the beef for more than two hours, however, you'll need to thaw it slightly for around 10 minutes before it can be sliced.

Serves 4
Cooking time: 1 hour 30 minutes
plus 2 hours freezing time

Carpaccio

300g of beef fillet

½ tsp coriander seeds

1 tsp juniper berries

½ tsp black peppercorns

½ tsp flaky sea salt

1 tsp Dijon mustard

1 tsp extra virgin olive oil, plus extra for drizzling

1 dash of vegetable oil

Pickled shallots

50ml of red wine vinegar

50ml of water

1 tbsp caster sugar

1 banana shallot, finely sliced into rings

Parmesan mayonnaise

1 egg yolk

1 tsp Dijon mustard

75ml of vegetable oil

25ml of extra virgin olive oil

1 tsp white wine vinegar

15g of Parmesan, finely grated

To serve

1 pear

20g of walnuts, toasted and roughly chopped

Micro cress, or baby leaves

Begin by marinating the beef. Toast the spices in a hot, dry pan for 30 seconds or until fragrant. Use a pestle and mortar to grind them into a coarse powder with the salt. Rub the beef fillet with the mustard and olive oil, then roll the beef in the ground spices. Wrap tightly in cling film and chill for 1 hour.

Meanwhile, make the pickled shallots. Add the vinegar, water, sugar and a pinch of salt to a saucepan and gently heat until the sugar dissolves. Remove from the heat, add the shallot and set aside until ready to use (leave for at least 1 hour).

Take the beef out of the fridge and remove the cling film. Place a heavy frying pan over a high heat and wait until it is smoking hot. Add a dash of oil and sear the beef all over – work quickly as you only want to sear the exterior. Once browned, wrap tightly in cling film once more. Place in the freezer for 2 hours.

While the beef freezes, make the mayonnaise. Whisk the egg yolk and mustard together until pale, then slowly drizzle in both oils whilst constantly whisking to emulsify – if it begins to split, add a splash of cold water. Stir in the vinegar and Parmesan, then season to taste with salt. Transfer to a piping bag if you have one and reserve in the fridge until needed.

Once the beef is semi-frozen, unwrap it from the cling film and use a sharp serrated knife to slice it against the grain as finely as possible – try to work quickly, as the warmer the beef is the harder it is to slice finely. Arrange the slices onto 4 serving plates, then place in the fridge until ready to serve.

20 minutes before serving, take the plates out of the fridge to allow them to come to room temperature. Drizzle over some extra virgin olive oil and scatter over the walnuts and pickled shallot rings. Peel and finely dice the pear and add to the plates, then add dots of the Parmesan mayonnaise. Finish with some cress or baby leaves.

Broccoli, leek and sun-blushed tomato tartlets

Broccoli and leek are slowly roasted with plenty of lemon and garlic to produce the deeply flavourful filling of these little tarts. The vegetables are blitzed into a pâté with basil then used to fill flaky puff pastry, topped with tomatoes and pine nuts for sweetness and crunch. You can make the pâté a day in advance.

Serves 6
Cooking time: 1 hour 30 minutes
Equipment: Food processor, 10cm round cutter, 9cm round cutter

150g of broccoli, florets roughly chopped and stem finely diced

1 leek, white part only, washed and sliced

2 garlic cloves, bashed but with their skins left on

1 lemon

2 tbsp olive oil, plus extra for dressing

1 handful of basil leaves

1 dash of white wine vinegar

1 sheet of puff pastry

1 egg, beaten with a pinch of salt

6 sun-blushed tomatoes, sliced into strips

2 tbsp pine nuts

Pea shoots, to serve

Preheat an oven to 200°C. Place the broccoli, leek and garlic cloves into a baking dish, then quarter the lemon and squeeze in the juice. Nestle the squeezed lemon quarters in amongst the vegetables, then toss everything with the olive oil and season with lots of salt and pepper. Cover the dish with foil then roast in the oven for 45 minutes.

Remove the foil from the dish, discard the lemon quarters and squeeze the garlic cloves out of their skins, discarding the skin. Place everything into a food processor along with the basil and pulse until the mixture comes together into a coarsely textured pâté – you may need to add some water to loosen the mixture a little. Season to taste with salt, pepper and a dash of vinegar.

Place a large baking tray into the oven (still at 200°C) to heat up. Place your sheet of puff pastry on a work surface and cut out 6 circles using a 10cm round cutter. Transfer them to a baking tray lined with baking paper. Use a 9cm round cutter to create a thin border around each circle – you want to cut very slightly into the pastry but not all the way through. Use a fork to prick small holes in the centre of each circle (but not the border), then brush with the egg wash.

Add a spoonful of the broccoli mixture to each tartlet, spreading it evenly but leaving the border clear. Carefully remove the hot baking tray from the oven and gently slide the baking paper from the cold tray to the hot one, with the tartlets on top. Bake for 10 minutes, until the borders around each tartlet puff up and start to turn golden.

Turn the oven down to 180°C and add strips of sun-blushed tomatoes and a few pine nuts to the top of each tartlet. Return to the oven for a further 5-8 minutes, until the tomatoes just begin to char lightly.

To serve, place a tartlet on each serving dish alongside a few pea shoots dressed in olive oil.

Chilled leek and potato soup with leek oil and leek hay

A clever take on French Vichyssoise which uses every part of the leek, this make-ahead chilled soup is perfect for the warmer months and is given a fine dining twist thanks to a bright green leek oil (made with the green tops) and crispy leek 'hay'. You can make everything the day before if desired.

Serves 4
Cooking time: 1 hour
plus chilling time
Equipment: Blender

350g of leeks

50g of unsalted butter

250g of floury potatoes, peeled and roughly chopped

600ml of vegetable stock

1 bay leaf

200g of vegetable oil, plus extra for deep-frying

100g of crème fraîche

100g of whole milk

1 lemon

Halve the leeks at the point where they turn from green to white. Roughly chop the green parts and place in a bowl of water so any dirt rises to the top. Peel the outer layer of the white leeks and set aside to make the 'hay' later. Finely slice the remaining white part of the leeks.

Melt the butter in a saucepan and add a pinch of salt. Stir in the finely sliced leeks and cook for 6 minutes, or until soft. Add the potatoes and cook for a few more minutes, then add the stock and bay leaf and gently simmer for 25 minutes.

Meanwhile, drain the green parts of the leeks. Bring a small pan of water to the boil and blanch the green leeks for 2 minutes, then plunge into iced water. Squeeze them in a j-cloth to remove any excess water – you want them to be as dry as possible. Transfer to a blender with the vegetable oil and blitz for 5 minutes, or until the oil turns bright green. Place a fine sieve over a bowl and line the sieve with a j-cloth. Pour the oil into the j-cloth – the oil will strain into the bowl below.

To make the leek hay, divide the reserved outer layers of the leeks in half. Cut half into very fine matchsticks against the grain, and the other half into very fine matchsticks with the grain. Fill a small pan with vegetable oil until at least 2cm deep, then heat to 180°C. Working in batches, deep-fry the leek strands until light brown (don't let them get too dark as they will taste bitter). Drain on kitchen paper and season with salt.

Once the soup has been cooking for 25 minutes, blitz in a blender until smooth. Stir in the crème fraîche, then add the milk until the soup is the consistency of double cream. Season to taste with lemon juice, salt and pepper, then refrigerate until completely chilled.

When ready to serve, pour the chilled soup into serving bowls, then drizzle with the green leek oil. Finish with a nest of the leek hay in the centre.

Chicken liver parfait with plum relish

It graces many a traditional restaurant menu, but chicken liver parfait is ideal for dinner parties at home as it can be made entirely in advance. Here, the rich buttery flavour is cut with a sweet and piquant plum relish – a match made in classical cookery heaven.

Serves 8
Cooking time: 1 hour 10 minutes
plus cooling time
Equipment: Blender

Parfait

200g of unsalted butter, softened

40g of shallots, sliced

1 garlic clove

2 juniper berries, crushed

2 sprigs of thyme

25ml of Madeira

50ml of port

200g of chicken livers, trimmed of any sinew and washed

1 egg

Sourdough, toasted, to serve

Plum relish

1 tbsp vegetable oil

75g of red onion, sliced

1 large plum, stone removed and diced into 1cm cubes

40ml of port

2 tbsp caster sugar

1 tsp red wine vinegar

1 clove

1 juniper berry

¼ star anise

2 black peppercorns

Place a pan over a medium heat and add a tablespoon of the butter. Once melted, add the shallot and garlic with a pinch of salt and cook for 5 minutes, until soft. Add the juniper, thyme, Madeira and port, bring the mixture to a simmer then cook until syrupy (around 10 minutes). Set aside to cool completely.

Preheat an oven to 150°C. Place the livers in a blender with the egg and the cooled port mixture (discard the thyme). Blitz until smooth, then add 75g of the remaining butter and blitz again until incorporated. Season with salt, then divide between 8 small (or 4 larger) ramekins.

Place the ramekins in a high-sided baking tray and boil a kettle. Place circles of baking paper on top of each ramekin so they lay flat against the parfait (this stops them turning brown), then pour the hot water into the tray so it reaches halfway up the ramekins. Place the tray into the oven and cook for 35 minutes.

While the parfaits cook, make the relish. Add the oil to a small saucepan over a medium heat, then cook the red onion with a pinch of salt for 5 minutes until soft. Add the plum, port, sugar and vinegar and turn the heat down to low.

Place the clove, juniper berry, star anise and peppercorns in a pestle and mortar or spice grinder and grind to a powder. Add this to the relish, then continue to gently cook until thick and syrupy. Give it a taste and add more sugar or salt if you think it needs it, then reserve in the fridge until needed.

Once the parfaits have cooked, take them out of the oven and leave to cool slightly. Meanwhile, gently melt the remaining butter. Peel off the baking paper then pour the melted butter into each ramekin. Place in the fridge for at least 1 hour to set.

To serve, bring the relish and parfaits out of the fridge 20 minutes before eating to allow them to come to room temperature. Serve with toasted sourdough.

Potted shrimp in herb and lemon butter

Looking for something simple to kick off a dinner party? Potted shrimp are the perfect make-ahead starter. Bolstered with fresh herbs and lemon, make sure the bread you're serving them with is top-quality to do the shrimp justice. This recipe can also be used to make an incredible sauce for fish.

Serves 4
Cooking time: 25 minutes
plus cooling time

150g of unsalted butter

1 lemon

½ banana shallot

150g of brown shrimp

5g of dill, leaves picked and finely chopped

5g of parsley, leaves picked and finely chopped

5g of tarragon, leaves picked and finely chopped

Good bread, to serve

Place the butter in a saucepan with a pinch of salt over a medium heat. Cook until the butter melts and has turned a golden, nutty brown colour. Pass through a fine sieve into a bowl to remove some of the larger milk solids.

Zest the lemon into the butter, then use a small knife to top and tail the lemon and carefully carve off the peel, trying to remove as much white pith as possible as you do so. Slice out 3 of the lemon segments, removing any remaining white pith, then add these to the warm butter and stir. The segments should break down into individual pearls.

Very finely chop the shallot and add it to the butter along with the brown shrimp. By now the butter should have cooled down and started to solidify slightly – if you work fast and it's still hot, wait a little longer until it's cool. Stir in the chopped herbs and season to taste with salt, pepper and a little more lemon juice if needed.

Transfer the mixture to 4 small serving bowls or ramekins and place in the fridge. An hour before you want to serve, take them out of the fridge so they come to room temperature. Serve with bread, toasted if desired.

Citrus-cured whiting with curried yoghurt and pickled cucumber

Curing fish changes its texture, allows any aromatics in the mixture to permeate throughout and ensures its natural flavour shines through. This starter of cured whiting, served with slices of pickled cucumber, dots of curried yoghurt and diced dried apricot is bright, colourful and incredibly fresh.

Serves 4
Cooking time: 30 minutes
plus 2-3 hours curing and pickling time

Cured whiting

2 whiting fillets, or cod fillets, skin-on and pin-boned (roughly 200g total)

80g of flaky sea salt

40g of caster sugar

1 lemon, zested

1 lime, zested

½ orange, zested

½ grapefruit, zested

Pickled cucumber

1 baby cucumber, or 40g of cucumber

30g of white wine vinegar

30g of water

1 tsp caster sugar

Curried yoghurt

50g of Greek-style yoghurt

1 tsp curry powder

¼ tsp turmeric powder

1 squeeze of lemon juice

To serve

2 dried apricots, finely diced

1 handful of coriander leaves, placed in a bowl of iced water to crisp up

1 lemon, zested

Extra virgin olive oil, for drizzling

Begin by curing the whiting 2-3 hours before serving. Mix together the salt, sugar and citrus zests, then sprinkle one-third of the mixture onto a tray. Place the fish skin-side down on top, then sprinkle over the rest of the curing mixture, packing it down onto the fish and ensuring it is completely covered. Cover and leave to cure for 2-3 hours, depending on the thickness of the fillet.

At the same time, pour the white wine vinegar, water, sugar and a pinch of salt into a small saucepan and heat until the sugar dissolves. Finely slice the cucumber and add it to the pan, then place in the fridge to pickle for 2-3 hours.

Mix together the yoghurt, curry powder and turmeric, then squeeze in a little lemon juice and stir in a pinch of salt. Reserve in the fridge until needed.

When ready to serve, wash the curing mixture off the fish and pat dry. Finely slice the fish on an angle, removing it from the skin as you do so, then arrange in a flat layer on serving plates.

Drain the pickled cucumber and add it on top, then sprinkle over the diced apricots. Give the yoghurt a quick mix if it has separated, then either spoon it over the fish or transfer to a piping bag to create little dots. Finish with lemon zest, coriander leaves and a drizzle of olive oil.

Salmon tartare with sour cream, burnt apple purée, capers and dill

Fresh, sweet and delicate, this salmon tartare is full of pure, clean flavours and topped with a burnt apple purée which adds a deep, caramelised complexity. Make the purée and prepare the tartare in advance, so you only need to plate up before serving.

Serves 4
Cooking time: 1 hour
Equipment: Blender, piping bag, 8cm metal ring

Salmon tartare

400g of salmon fillet, as fresh as possible, skinned

20g of capers, drained

1 green apple

2 lemons, zested and juiced

1 bunch of dill, fronds picked

80g of sour cream

Burnt apple purée

2 green apples

20g of unsalted butter, softened

10g of demerara sugar

Preheat an oven to 200°C. Quarter and core the apples for the purée, then place on a baking tray. Mix together the butter and demerara sugar, then spread this on the apple quarters, covering them completely. Transfer to the oven and cook for 30 minutes, or until the apples are deeply caramelised and beginning to blacken.

Tip the burnt apples into a blender with a splash of water and blitz until smooth. Leave to cool, then pass through a fine sieve and transfer to a piping bag.

Dice the salmon into 1cm cubes and roughly chop the capers. Peel and core the apple, then finely dice into 5cm cubes. Coat a quarter of the diced apple in a little lemon juice, then set aside along with some of the dill fronds to garnish.

Finely chop the remaining dill, then combine with the capers, salmon and the remaining three-quarters of apple. Add the sour cream and the lemon zest. Stir to combine then season to taste with salt, pepper and lemon juice.

To serve, use an 8cm metal ring to create a neat circle of the salmon tartare on each plate. Pipe dots of the burnt apple purée on top and finish with the reserved dill fronds and apple.

Twice-baked Lancashire cheese soufflés
by Shaun Hill

A dish which has stood the test of time, these soufflés eliminate any last-minute nerves about rising as they're baked twice – once in advance, another just before serving. Garnish them with a side salad or sprinkle over some extra cheese if desired. They're an ideal starter to serve before Shaun's equally impressive chicken recipe on p154.

Serves 6
Cooking time: 45 minutes
plus cooling time
Equipment: Electric whisk,
6 ramekins

25g of unsalted butter, softened, plus extra for greasing

25g of plain flour

175ml of whole milk

3 eggs, separated

3g of cornflour

125g of Lancashire cheese, ideally Lancashire Bomb, crumbled

4g of English mustard

4g of Worcestershire sauce

1 dash of Tabasco sauce

Parmesan, or any cheese you like, finely grated, to serve

Preheat an oven to 180°C. Grease 6 ramekins or bowls with butter then place them in the fridge to set.

Mix together the butter and flour to create a thick dough-like paste called a beurre manié. Warm the milk in a pan then whisk in the paste as it comes to the boil. As soon as it boils remove the pan from the heat, leave to cool for 5 minutes, then whisk in the egg yolks and cornflour.

Use an electric whisk to whip the egg whites into stiff peaks, then carefully fold these into the thickened milk along with the Lancashire cheese, mustard, Worcestershire and Tabasco sauces and a pinch of salt and pepper.

Spoon the mixture into the ramekins or bowls then place them in a deep roasting tray. Fill the tray with hot water so the water comes halfway up the sides of the ramekins, then place in the oven for 15 minutes. Remove the tray from the oven, lift the ramekins out of the water and leave to cool, then cover with cling film and keep in the fridge until needed.

When ready to serve, ensure the oven is preheated to 180°C. Carefully remove the soufflés from the ramekins, running a knife around the edge of them if needed to help loosen. Transfer them to a baking tray and place the ramekins back in the oven for 8 minutes. Serve with salad and/or plenty of extra cheese grated over the top.

Honey-glazed quail with mixed seed scratchings and sriracha mayonnaise
by Kerth Gumbs

A whole quail always looks impressive on the plate – when they're glazed and cooked over a fierce heat, however, they really come into their own. Kerth Gumbs pairs them with a sriracha mayonnaise for dipping and a crunchy mixture of seeds and bacon for texture. Serve it before Kerth's stuffed red mullet on p157.

Serves 6
Cooking time: 1 hour 10 minutes
Equipment: Blender

Quail

6 quail

4 garlic cloves, finely chopped

3 lemons, juiced

2 oranges, juiced

1 tsp garlic powder

½ tsp paprika

60ml of olive oil

2 sprigs of thyme

Glaze

40g of honey

25ml of light soy sauce

3 tbsp water

½ garlic clove, finely chopped

1 bay leaf

Sriracha mayonnaise

60g of ketchup

30g of sriracha

15g of red onion, roughly chopped

½ lemon, juiced

1 sprig of coriander

130g of mayonnaise

Mixed seed scratchings

2 rashers of smoked streaky bacon

30g of pumpkin seeds, toasted

15g of sunflower seeds, toasted

1 small handful of pork scratchings, roughly chopped (optional)

½ lemon, zested

Begin by making the sriracha mayonnaise. Place the ketchup, sriracha, red onion, lemon juice and coriander sprig in a blender and blitz until smooth. Pass through a fine sieve, then whisk in the mayonnaise. Season to taste with salt, then transfer to a squeezy bottle if you have one and store in the fridge.

Preheat an oven to 180°C. Place the bacon for the scratchings mixture onto a tray and cook in the oven for 5 minutes. Remove from the oven, dice into small, crumb-sized pieces, then return to the oven for a few more minutes until crisp and dark. Mix with the rest of the ingredients for the scratchings and place in an airtight container until needed.

Pour all the ingredients for the glaze into a small saucepan and bring to the boil. Cook for 3 minutes, then remove from the heat and leave to infuse.

For the quail, you need to spatchcock each bird. Using a strong pair of scissors, cut down each side of the backbone and remove, then cut a slit into each of the thighs and carefully remove the thigh bones. Flip the bird over then push down to flatten. Repeat with the remaining quail, then place in a large bowl with the rest of the ingredients and a pinch of salt. Set aside in the fridge for at least 20 minutes to marinate.

To cook the quail on the barbecue, thread them onto skewers, brush liberally with the glaze and cook for around 3 minutes each side over a fierce heat, brushing with more glaze as they cook. Alternatively, heat a griddle pan until smoking hot, add a dash of oil then cook the quail skin-side down for 3 minutes. Brush liberally with the glaze all over, then lower the heat and flip the quail, adding more glaze and swirling the pan to stop the glaze from burning too much. Cook for a further 3 minutes.

To serve, place the quail on serving plates and sprinkle with the scratchings. Pipe or spoon a large dot of the sriracha mayonnaise alongside.

Seared scallops with Thai salad and peanut tuile
by Mark Dodson

British waters are home to the best scallops in the world, which is why they always fill us with excitement when we see them on the plate. Simply fried over a fierce heat until just warm in the centre, Mark Dodson serves them with an Asian-style slaw and a clever little peanut tuile. This starter matches exquisitely with Mark's salt-baked sea bass dish on p159.

Serves 6
Cooking time: 1 hour
plus 4 hours marinating time

Scallops

18 scallops, as fresh and large as you can find

1 dash of vegetable oil

Salad

150g of Chinese cabbage, cored and finely shredded

4 spring onions, finely sliced

½ red chilli, finely chopped

5g of coriander leaves, chopped

15g of toasted flaked almonds

30ml of rice wine vinegar

30ml of vegetable oil

25ml of light soy sauce

25ml of fish sauce

30g of caster sugar

Tuile

25g of icing sugar

13g of plain flour

16g of orange juice

25g of smooth peanut butter

1 tsp sesame seeds

Begin by making the salad, as it needs at least 4 hours to marinate. Place the cabbage, spring onions, chilli, coriander leaves and almonds in a bowl. Pour the rest of the ingredients into a saucepan and gently heat until the sugar dissolves. Leave to cool completely, then pour over the cabbage mixture and toss thoroughly. Leave to infuse and marinate in the fridge for at least 4 hours, or overnight.

To make the tuiles, mix all of the ingredients together until well combined and smooth, then place in the fridge for 30 minutes to chill. Meanwhile, preheat an oven to 180°C.

Once the tuile mixture is cold, place a sheet of baking paper on a baking tray. Use a palette knife to spread the mixture onto the paper as thin as possible. Transfer the tray to the oven and bake the mixture for 5 minutes, then allow to cool slightly. Whilst still warm, carefully cut the baked mixture into long, thin rectangles. Allow to cool completely, then store in an airtight container until needed.

To cook the scallops, place a large frying pan over a high heat. If you don't like the orange coral on the scallops you can remove it, but it's delicious to eat. Pat the scallops dry and season with salt, then add a drizzle of oil to the pan. Place the scallops in the pan in a clockwise circle, cooking the best-looking side first. Placing them in a circle means you know which ones have had the longest cooking time. Cook for 3 minutes, then flip the scallops and cook for a further minute. Remove and set aside.

To serve, add a small mound of salad to each plate, then top with a tuile. Place 3 scallops alongside.

Dinner Party
Mains

Salt-baked celeriac with beetroot cashew cream and cavolo nero

After a vegan dish with a difference? This ethereal dish is what you're looking for. The bed of pastel pink cashew cream is silky and rich, topped with a crispy, earthy, perfectly seasoned slab of celeriac and iron-rich cavolo nero. Prepare the beetroot cream and bake the celeriac in advance.

Serves 4
Cooking time: 1 hour 30 minutes
Equipment: Blender

Celeriac

200g of salt

300g of plain flour, plus extra for dusting

2 tbsp rosemary leaves, finely chopped

150ml of warm water

1 large celeriac, scrubbed clean and larger roots removed

2 sheets of nori seaweed

2 tsp Marmite

2 tsp olive oil

50g of polenta

Beetroot cream

120g of cashews

250g of almond milk

2 sprigs of thyme

200g of cooked beetroot

10g of lemon juice

Cavolo nero

16 cavolo nero leaves

100ml of vegetable oil, plus extra for frying

1 banana shallot

1 pinch of chilli flakes

1 lemon, zested and juiced

Preheat an oven to 180°C. To make the salt dough, mix together the salt, flour, rosemary and warm water to create a dough. Dust a work surface with flour and roll out the dough until 1cm thick, then carefully wrap the celeriac with nori, splashing it with water to help it stick, followed by the dough. Place it on a tray seam-side down and bake for 1 hour.

Meanwhile, make the beetroot cream. Place the cashews in a pan with the almond milk and thyme and bring to a simmer. Cook for 10 minutes, then pick out the thyme sprigs and transfer the milk and nuts to a blender. Add the beetroot (plus any juices from the packet) and blitz until thick, smooth and pink. Season to taste with salt and the lemon juice. Set aside.

Strip the cavolo nero leaves from their stems, then roughly chop the stems. Pour the vegetable oil into a heavy saucepan and heat until shimmering, then fry the stems for 3-5 minutes, or until crisp. Drain on kitchen paper and season with salt.

Mix together the Marmite and oil and pour the polenta onto a plate. Cut open the salt crust around the celeriac and discard, along with the nori. Slice the celeriac into 4 steaks, then paint them liberally with the Marmite and coat with the polenta.

Bring a pan of salted water to the boil and place a large frying pan over a medium heat. Add a dash of oil to the frying pan followed by the celeriac slices and fry for 3-5 minutes on both sides until crisp.

Meanwhile, cook the cavolo nero leaves in the water for 3 minutes, then drain. Place another frying pan over a medium heat with a splash of oil, then cook the shallot and chilli flakes for 3 minutes. Add the leaves along with some lemon juice and zest then toss to combine. Season with salt.

To serve, spread a bed of beetroot cream onto each plate, then add a celeriac steak and top with the leaves and crispy stems.

Duck breast with turnip gratin and rhubarb ketchup

A hearty, wintry dish of duck, turnips, rhubarb and beetroot that's perfect for those frosty first few months of the year, this recipe shows just how tasty turnips can be (although the generous amount of cream, cheese and bacon certainly helps things along). The ketchup is a great fridge staple to have on hand – try it slathered in a bacon sandwich.

Serves 4
Cooking time: 1 hour 30 minutes
Equipment: Blender

4 duck breasts

200g of Tenderstem broccoli

Extra virgin olive oil, for drizzling

Gratin

450g of turnips (roughly 5 large turnips)

1 tsp vegetable oil

5 rashers of smoked streaky bacon, roughly chopped

200ml of whole milk

200ml of double cream

2 garlic cloves, grated

2 bay leaves

50g of Gruyère cheese, grated

Rhubarb ketchup

1 star anise

2 juniper berries

1 clove

1 tbsp vegetable oil

½ onion, diced

½-inch piece of ginger, peeled and diced

200g of rhubarb, sliced

25ml of red wine vinegar

75g of caster sugar

80g of cooked beetroot

Begin by making the ketchup, as this can be done in advance. Place the star anise, juniper berries and clove in a spice grinder or pestle and mortar and grind to a powder. Heat the oil in a saucepan and gently cook the onion and ginger with a pinch of salt for 5 minutes, or until soft. Add the rhubarb to the pan and cook for another 5 minutes, stirring occasionally, until it becomes slightly mushy. Stir in the vinegar, sugar and ground spices then cook over a low heat for 5 minutes.

Add the contents of the pan to a blender with the beetroot and blitz until smooth. Season to taste with salt and more vinegar or sugar if it needs it. Reserve in the fridge (in a squeezy bottle if you have one).

Preheat an oven to 180°C. Peel the turnips, then use a sharp knife or mandoline to slice them into very thin discs. Fry the bacon in a saucepan with the oil until beginning to crisp, then pour in the milk, cream, garlic and bay leaves. Bring to the boil, remove from the heat and pass through a fine sieve into a jug. Discard the bay leaves but reserve the bacon.

Place a layer of the turnip discs into the base of a deep ovenproof dish. Scatter over some of the bacon, then continue layering up the turnips with bacon scattered between each layer. Pour the strained cream into the dish, then sprinkle the grated cheese on top. Bake in the oven for 35 minutes.

Score the skin of each duck breast diagonally, with 5mm gaps between each cut. Sprinkle with salt, then place skin-side down in a cold ovenproof frying pan. When the gratin has around 15 minutes left to cook, place the pan over a medium heat and cook for 5 minutes, or until the fat has rendered out and the skin has turned golden.

Recipe continues overleaf

Recipe continued

Transfer the pan to the oven and cook for another 5 minutes for a medium-rare finish (add another few minutes if you like your duck more well-done). Meanwhile, bring a pan of salted water to the boil.

When the duck and gratin have finished cooking, remove from the oven and leave to rest for 5 minutes. Meanwhile, plunge the Tenderstem broccoli into the boiling water and cook for 5 minutes, then drain and drizzle with extra virgin olive oil and plenty of black pepper.

To serve, slice the gratin into 4 pieces and divide between plates. Carve each duck breast in half lengthways and place alongside, with some broccoli and a spoonful or dot of ketchup.

Black pudding-stuffed lamb saddle with braised lettuce and red onions

The perfect recipe to test your butchery skills, stuffing and rolling a lamb saddle might sound intimidating but it's easier than you'd think. The trimmings are chopped into lardons to go with the braised lettuce, ensuring nothing goes to waste. You can also prep and stuff the saddle well in advance, avoiding any last-minute stress on the day you plan to serve.

Serves 6
Cooking time: 2 hours 15 minutes
plus resting time
Equipment: Food processor, butcher's string

Lamb saddle

1 lamb saddle, boned and fillets removed and reserved (ask your butcher to do this for you)

50g of chicken breast

40g of black pudding, roughly chopped

40g of double cream

4 chives, finely chopped

1 dash of vegetable oil

Braised lettuce

3 romaine lettuces, washed and quartered

500ml of chicken stock, or fresh lamb stock

150g of frozen peas

1 sprig of mint, leaves picked and chopped

1 lemon, zested

Roast onions

9 small red onions

1 tbsp olive oil

1 tbsp balsamic vinegar

2 tsp honey

Begin by stuffing the lamb, as this can be done in advance. Place the chicken breast in a food processor and blitz to a paste. With the motor running, add the black pudding and then the double cream and wait until the mixture becomes smooth – try not to overmix as the cream might split. Fold in the chives and season heavily with salt and pepper.

Place the saddle skin-side down with the loins vertical in front of you. The flaps at either sides of the loins are the lamb belly – cut along the left-hand side of the left loin to remove this piece of belly and reserve. On the right-hand side, place your knife flat against the board on top of the belly flap and carefully trim away any extra fat, leaving you with a thin, even flap about 3mm thick for rolling the saddle up with. Reserve the trimmings with the other piece of belly you removed.

Spoon the blended stuffing between the loins, then arrange the reserved fillets on top and season with plenty of salt and pepper. Roll the saddle tightly, using the thin flap of lamb belly to help create a seal. Use butcher's string to tie the lamb up tightly and keep everything in place, looping the string around 5 times to mark 6 even portions. Wrap tightly in cling film, then place in the fridge for at least 1 hour to firm up.

Take the reserved piece of lamb belly and use a sharp knife to remove the tough outer membrane. Chop the belly and the reserved trimmings into lardons, then place in the fridge.

Around 1½ hours before you plan to serve, preheat an oven to 200°C. Peel and quarter the red onions, keeping the root attached so the wedges stay together. Place them in a small baking dish, then drizzle with the olive oil, balsamic vinegar and a little salt. Cover with foil and roast for 40 minutes.

Recipe continues overleaf

Recipe continued

As soon as the onions have gone in, place an ovenproof frying pan over a high heat and remove the cling film from the lamb. Add a dash of vegetable oil to the pan and brown the saddle all over for 6-8 minutes, until well caramelised. Transfer to the oven and cook for a further 35 minutes (or longer if you don't like your lamb a little pink).

Meanwhile, prepare the braised lettuce. Place a large frying pan over a medium heat and add the lamb lardons. Once the fat has rendered out and they begin to crisp up, push them to the side and add the lettuce, cut-side down, frying for a few minutes until lightly caramelised. Pour in the stock and peas, then leave to simmer for 10 minutes. Stir in the mint and lemon zest, then set aside to reheat before serving.

Once the lamb is cooked, remove it from the oven and leave to rest for 15 minutes. Take out the onions, remove the foil, then drizzle over the honey. Return them to the oven for another 15 minutes, or until glazed and starting to crisp up a little.

To serve, gently reheat and divide the braised lettuce (along with some of the liquid) between 6 wide bowls. Snip the butcher's string off the lamb and carve into 6 portions, then place these on top. Garnish with the roasted onions.

Chicken schnitzel with anchovy-fried potatoes and gremolata

Schnitzels are good for two reasons: they're delicious and give us a chance to expel some pent-up energy by bashing something with a rolling pin. Served with some stunning potatoes fried in anchovy oil and a fresh, zesty gremolata to lighten the flavours, this is a quick, easy dish that's guaranteed to please.

Serves 4
Cooking time: 1 hour

Schnitzels

4 chicken breasts, skinless

80g of plain flour

2 small eggs, beaten with a dash of milk and a pinch of salt

2 tsp Dijon mustard

200g of fine panko breadcrumbs

Vegetable oil, for frying

Anchovy-fried potatoes

1kg of floury potatoes, such as Maris Pipers

1 tin of anchovy fillets in olive oil

Pickled shallots

50ml of red wine vinegar

50ml of water

1 tbsp caster sugar

1 banana shallot, finely sliced into rings

Gremolata

10 sprigs of parsley, leaves picked and finely chopped

4 tbsp capers, drained and finely chopped

1 gherkin, drained and finely chopped

1 lemon, zested

To serve

100g of watercress

Mayonnaise

Bring a pan of salted water to the boil. Peel the potatoes and dice into 2cm cubes. Add them to the water and cook for 15 minutes, or until tender. Drain and leave to steam-dry.

Meanwhile, pickle the shallots by heating the vinegar, water, sugar and a pinch of salt in a pan until the sugar dissolves. Remove from the heat, add the shallot rings and set aside.

Butterfly each chicken breast by cutting it lengthways almost in half. Lay the breast out between 2 sheets of baking paper, then use a rolling pin to bash it flat. Repeat with the other breasts.

Set up a breadcrumbing station by placing the flour on a wide plate, then a wide bowl with the eggs and mustard whisked together, followed by a final plate of breadcrumbs. Ensure you have a tray to lay the crumbed chicken on at the end. Dust each flattened chicken breast in flour, then coat in egg, then in breadcrumbs. For an extra-crispy schnitzel dip them in the egg and breadcrumbs again. Reserve on the tray.

Preheat an oven to 100°C and place a large frying pan over a high heat. Add the anchovies (along with their oil) to the frying pan and fry until they begin to break down, then tip in the potatoes. Fry, stirring occasionally, for 10 minutes, until the potatoes are crisp. Transfer to the oven to keep warm.

Place 2 frying pans over a medium-high heat and add 2 tablespoons of vegetable oil to each one. Once hot, add a schnitzel to each pan, then cook for 4 minutes each side until golden and crisp. Transfer to the oven to keep warm, then repeat with the remaining schnitzels.

Make the gremolata by mixing together all the ingredients. To serve, place a schnitzel on each plate. Sprinkle the gremolata over the schnitzels, then add some anchovy potatoes and pickled shallots on top. Finish with some mayonnaise and the watercress on the side.

Cheddar gnocchi with asparagus and tomato and olive salsa

Gnocchi are comforting little pillows of goodness, often served with rich, thick sauces to combat chilly weather. In this recipe they're bolstered with cheddar, before being served in a fresh springtime salsa of asparagus, tomato, olive and basil with the pleasing tartness of sherry vinegar bringing everything together.

Serves 4
Cooking time: 1 hour 45 minutes

Gnocchi

450g of floury potatoes, such as Maris Pipers

50g of cheddar, very finely grated

125g of 00 flour, plus extra for dusting

1 egg yolk

Salsa

1 small garlic clove, finely grated

60g of pitted green olives, finely chopped

200g of cherry tomatoes, finely chopped

1 spring onion, finely sliced

4 sprigs of basil, leaves picked and chopped

10g of Parmesan, or vegetarian Italian hard cheese, finely grated

60g of extra virgin olive oil, plus extra for drizzling

1 dash of sherry vinegar

To serve

50g of unsalted butter

150g of asparagus, trimmed and cut into batons

Preheat an oven to 180°C. Pierce the potatoes with a knife, then place them on a tray and into the oven for 1 hour, or until completely cooked through.

Allow the potatoes to cool slightly. Whilst they're still very warm, slice them in half, scoop out the flesh then pass the flesh through a potato ricer or fine sieve to create a dry, fluffy mash. Scatter the potato onto a work surface and sprinkle over the grated cheddar and flour. Place the egg yolk in the middle, then use a dough cutter or knife to 'chop' the ingredients together evenly – this stops the gluten in the flour from being overworked which can result in chewy gnocchi. Once worked together into an even rubble, use your hands to gently bring the mixture together into a smooth dough.

Dust the work surface lightly with flour and divide the dough into 6. Roll each piece into a sausage around 2cm in diameter, then cut the dough into 2cm pieces. Using a gnocchi board or the tines of a fork, gently press grooves into each gnocchi, then place on a tray and set aside.

Mix together the garlic, olives, tomatoes, spring onion, basil, Parmesan and olive oil in a bowl, then season to taste with salt, pepper and a splash of sherry vinegar.

Bring 2 pans of salted water to the boil and place a large non-stick frying pan over a medium heat. Once the water is boiling, add the butter to the frying pan and add the gnocchi, working in batches, to 1 of the pans of water. Cook the gnocchi for 1 minute, or until they start to stand up on the bottom of the pan. Lift them out with a slotted spoon and transfer them to the frying pan, then cook until lightly golden and crisp.

When all the gnocchi are in the frying pan, cook the asparagus in the second pan of boiling water for 2-3 minutes. Drain and add to the gnocchi, turn the heat down, then add the dressing to gently warm through. Divide between bowls and serve.

Hake with caramelised cauliflower purée and braised cabbage

Hake is woefully underused here in the UK, but in places like Spain it's held in high regard. Make the most of its meaty texture and delicate flavour by pairing it with a sweet, nutty cauliflower purée, soft and crunchy cabbage and a knockout sauce full of toasty butter, capers and hazelnuts.

Serves 4
Cooking time: 1 hour 25 minutes
Equipment: Blender

Hake

4 hake fillets, weighing approx. 150g each

2 tbsp vegetable oil

Purée

500g of cauliflower, florets roughly chopped and stalk finely sliced

100g of unsalted butter

100ml of dry sherry

200ml of water

1 tbsp sherry vinegar

Cabbage

1 small hispi cabbage

1 tbsp vegetable oil

300g of chicken stock

Sauce

40g of unsalted butter

20g of capers, drained

20g of hazelnuts, roughly chopped

1 lemon, juiced

Begin with the cauliflower purée. Add the cauliflower to a large saucepan with the butter and place over a low heat. Cook for 30 minutes, stirring regularly, or until the cauliflower has turned a dark golden brown. Add the sherry to deglaze, then bring to a simmer and cook for another 5 minutes to reduce. Pour in the water and simmer for another 5-10 minutes, or until the cauliflower is completely soft.

Transfer the contents of the pan to a blender and add the sherry vinegar. Blitz until completely smooth, adding more water if needed, then season to taste with salt, pepper and a touch more sherry vinegar if it needs it. Transfer to a pan and cover, ready to reheat later.

Preheat an oven to 80°C and place a large non-stick frying pan over a high heat. Cut the cabbage into quarters through the root, so the wedges stay intact. Add the vegetable oil to the pan then place the cabbage quarters cut-side down. Cook for 6 minutes, flipping onto the other cut side halfway through, until they are deep brown and beginning to char.

Pour in the chicken stock, turn down the heat and cover. Cook for 5 minutes, then lift the cabbages out of the stock and transfer to a tray, keeping them warm in the oven. Pour the remaining chicken stock into a small saucepan, then leave to simmer and reduce by around a third.

Give the frying pan a quick wash, then place it back over a high heat. Pat the skin of the hake fillets dry to ensure crispy skin, then season with salt and pepper. Add the oil to the pan and place the fish skin-side down. Turn the heat down to medium and cook for 4-5 minutes, until the skin is golden and crisp. Meanwhile, gently reheat the purée.

Recipe continues overleaf

Recipe continued

Add the butter, capers and hazelnuts to the pan and baste the fish for a minute, then carefully flip the fillets over and baste for another 30 seconds. Turn off the heat, lift the fish out of the pan and set aside to rest.

Pour everything else left in the pan into the reduced chicken stock, then season to taste with plenty of lemon juice and salt if it needs it (the chicken stock may be salty enough already).

To serve, divide the purée between 4 plates and spread out using the back of a spoon to create a neat circle. Place the hake and cabbage on top, then finish with the sauce.

Pork chop with braised lentils, chimichurri and saffron aioli

Pork and lentils is a tried and tested combination, and this wonderfully nourishing dish sees the duo accompanied by a zingy chimichurri and rich aioli flavoured with saffron and rendered pork fat. You want big, thick chops for this dish, and while the rendering process does take a while, it's well worth it.

Serves 4
Cooking time: 1 hour 30 minutes
Equipment: Food processor

Pork chops

2 pork chops, roughly 250g each and at least 2.5cm thick, rind removed

2 tbsp vegetable oil

Lentils

1 tbsp olive oil

2 banana shallots, finely chopped

1 celery stick, finely chopped

3 garlic cloves, finely chopped

175ml of dry white wine

225g of green lentils, or puy lentils

500ml of pork stock, or water

2 sprigs of thyme

1 tbsp white wine vinegar

Chimichurri

1 small shallot, roughly chopped

2 handfuls of flat-leaf parsley leaves

1 handful of coriander leaves

5 oregano leaves

150ml of olive oil

75ml of red wine vinegar

1 pinch of chilli flakes (optional)

Saffron aioli

1 pinch of saffron

1 large egg yolk

1 tsp Dijon mustard

1 small garlic clove

50ml of vegetable oil

½ lemon, juiced

Score a criss-cross pattern deep into the fat all the way down the side of each chop. Balance the pork chops fat-side down in a cold ovenproof frying pan and place over a low heat to slowly render the fat (this should take 15-20 minutes). Pour the fat out of the pan occasionally into a bowl during this process and reserve – you will need 100ml to make the aioli, but if you don't get enough rendered fat you can make up the difference with vegetable oil. When most of the fat has rendered out, remove the chops from the pan and set aside to cook later.

Use the same frying pan to cook the lentils. Add the olive oil, then cook the shallot and celery for 5 minutes until soft. Add the garlic and cook for a couple of minutes, then deglaze the pan with the white wine.

Bring to a simmer and reduce by two-thirds, then add the lentils, stock, thyme and white wine vinegar and simmer for 15 minutes – the lentils should still have a little bite to them. Keep warm or reheat before serving.

Meanwhile, make the chimichurri by pounding the shallot into a coarse paste using a pestle and mortar. Gradually add the parsley leaves, pounding as you go, then do the same with the coriander and oregano. Stir in the olive oil and vinegar to create a loose sauce, then add the chilli flakes (if using). Season to taste with a pinch of salt and pepper and set aside.

Soak the saffron in a tablespoon of hot water for a couple of minutes. Combine the egg yolk, Dijon mustard, garlic and a pinch of salt in a food processor and blend for a minute or so until thick and pale.

Recipe continues overleaf

Recipe continued

Add the saffron and water, then with the motor still running, slowly drizzle in 100ml of the reserved pork fat. Follow that with the vegetable oil, then finish with the lemon juice. Taste the aioli and add any extra seasoning you think it needs.

When ready to serve, preheat an oven to 180°C. Place an ovenproof frying pan over a high heat and add a dash of vegetable oil. When smoking hot, season the chops with salt and pepper and sear for 1-2 minutes on each side until golden, then transfer to the oven and roast for 5 minutes, turning halfway through. Remove and leave to rest for a few minutes while you gently reheat the lentils.

To serve, carve the meat off the bone and slice. Spoon some lentils into a bowl, then arrange the pork over the top. Finish with a pinch of sea salt, a spoonful of the chimichurri and a dollop of aioli.

Chicken bourride
by Shaun Hill

Sauces are often thickened with flour or by reducing the liquid. In this wonderful recipe by Shaun Hill, however, a generous dollop of garlic aioli does the job which, as you can imagine, provides seriously tasty results. Bourride is typically a Provençal fish stew, but chicken works just as well to create a dish that's guaranteed to go down a storm.

Serves 4
Cooking time: 1 hour
Equipment: Blender

Chicken

4 tbsp vegetable oil

1 free-range chicken, jointed, or 8 bone-in chicken thighs

2 shallots, sliced

2 red chillies, deseeded and sliced

2 red peppers, deseeded and diced

100ml of white wine

400ml of chicken stock

½ orange, zested

1 large pinch of saffron

Aioli

2 egg yolks

3 large garlic cloves, finely grated

1 tbsp Dijon mustard

100ml of olive oil

150ml of vegetable oil

1 tbsp lemon juice

To serve

1 lemon, zested

1 handful of parsley leaves, chopped

Crusty bread, or boiled new potatoes

Place a wide, deep frying pan over a medium heat and add 2 tablespoons of the vegetable oil. Season the chicken pieces all over with salt and pepper, then add to the pan skin-side down and cook for 5 minutes, or until the skin crisps up and turns a deep golden colour. Remove the chicken from the pan and set aside on a plate.

In the same pan, add the remaining oil followed by the shallots, chillies and red peppers. Cook for 6-8 minutes, until softened but without colour. Pour in the wine, simmer for a few minutes, then add the chicken stock, orange zest and saffron. Simmer for 5 minutes, then pour the contents of the pan into a blender and blitz until smooth.

Pour the blended sauce back into the pan, then place the chicken pieces back in flesh-side down. Leave to simmer and braise for 25 minutes, or until the chicken is cooked through.

Meanwhile, make the aioli. Place the egg yolks, grated garlic and mustard in a bowl and whisk for a few minutes until the yolks are thick and pale. Slowly drizzle in the oils, whisking constantly, to form an emulsion. If the mixture begins to split, add a splash of cold water. Season to taste with salt, pepper and a splash of lemon juice. You can also create the aioli in a food processor if desired.

Once the chicken is cooked, lift it out of the sauce and set aside. Whisk the aioli into the sauce over a low heat for a few minutes until thickened and smooth.

To serve, you can simply place the chicken back into the sauce and bring it to the table, or divide the sauce between 4 bowls and arrange the chicken on top. Garnish with lemon zest, parsley and a crack of black pepper. Serve with crusty bread or potatoes to ensure none of the sauce goes to waste.

Red mullet with prawn mousse and sambal
by Kerth Gumbs

Red mullet is an incredible fish, with a meaty, robust flavour and texture. Here it's stuffed with prawn mousse and liberally dressed with a punchy, incredibly moreish sambal. A wonderful dish to serve when the sun is shining. If you can't find red mullet, then red snapper, sea bream or sea bass work well too. You'll have more sambal than you need for this recipe, but it keeps well in the fridge.

Serves 4
Cooking time: 1 hour 30 minutes
Equipment: Food processor

4 red mullet, weighing approx. 400g each, whole if filleting at home

3 sprigs of thyme, leaves picked

1 bunch of spring onions, halved and cut into very fine strips

1 bunch of Tenderstem broccoli

1 lemon, juiced

1 handful of roasted peanuts, roughly chopped, to garnish (optional)

Puffed rice

250ml of vegetable oil, for deep-frying, plus extra for cooking

30g of wild rice

Prawn mousse

150g of raw shelled prawns, roughly chopped

3g of sea salt

2 egg whites

100g of double cream

½ lemon, zested

½ bunch of chives, finely chopped

Begin by making the sambal, as this actually benefits from a day or so of infusing time. Place the shallots, garlic, ginger, tomato purée, salt, sugars, chillies, dried shrimp, stock cube and vegetable oil in a food processor and blitz into a paste. Add to a pan with the chopped tomatoes, then bring to a simmer over a medium heat. Cook for around 30 minutes, stirring regularly to prevent burning, until it reaches a jam-like consistency and smells incredibly fragrant.

Meanwhile, for the prawn mousse, place 100g of the prawns, the salt and the egg whites into a food processor and blitz for 30 seconds. With the motor still running, gradually pour in the double cream to create a smooth mousse. Transfer to a bowl, then stir through the lemon zest, chives and remaining prawns. Cover and reserve in the fridge until ready to use.

For the puffed rice, bring the vegetable oil to 190°C and add the wild rice, which should puff up in a minute or so. Drain on kitchen paper and season with salt, then place in an airtight container until needed.

After the sambal has been cooking for 30 minutes, add the ketchup, fish sauce, vinegar and peanut oil, cook for a further 2 minutes, then taste for seasoning. Allow to cool then store in the fridge until needed.

If your fish is whole and unprepared, you need to fillet it at home (if your mullet comes pre-filleted, ignore this step). Cut alongside either side of the spine, making a deep cut but ensuring you don't pierce the belly. Use a pair of scissors to cut away the spine at either end, then remove along with the guts of the fish. Rinse the mullet well in water, then pat dry with kitchen towel.

Ingredients continue overleaf

Recipe continues overleaf

Ingredients and recipe continued

Sambal

150g of shallots, roughly chopped

10g of garlic, roughly chopped

15g of fresh ginger, peeled and roughly chopped

40g of tomato purée

5g of sea salt

15g of palm sugar

15g of caster sugar

20g of red chilli, deseeded and roughly chopped

1 Scotch bonnet chilli

40g of dried shrimp

½ vegetable stock cube

150ml of vegetable oil

100g of tinned chopped tomatoes

30g of tomato ketchup

10ml of fish sauce

25ml of sherry vinegar

75ml of peanut oil

Fill the mullets with the prawn mousse, then place them on individual pieces of baking paper. Drizzle with oil, season with salt and pepper and sprinkle over the thyme leaves. Wrap the fish in the baking paper to cover, then cover again with another layer of tin foil. Place in the fridge until ready to cook.

Preheat an oven to 190°C. Place the wrapped fish in the oven and cook for 20-25 minutes. Submerge the sliced spring onions into iced water to crisp and curl up and and bring a pan of salted water to the boil..

Leave the fish to rest for 5 minutes before unwrapping them. Meanwhile, blanch the broccoli in the boiling water for 3 minutes until tender, then drain and slice on the angle. Season with salt, pepper and a squeeze of lemon juice.

To serve, place the stuffed fish onto serving dishes. Spoon the sambal onto the fish, then arrange the broccoli next to it with the spring onions. Sprinkle over the puffed rice and peanuts.

Salt-baked sea bass with lettuce, potatoes and chive beurre blanc
by Mark Dodson

A masterclass in classical cookery, this delicate dish of sea bass, potatoes in a buttery chive sauce and braised lettuce is perfect for celebratory meals. The salt crust, pancakes and lettuce can all be made in advance, meaning you only need to cook the fish, potatoes and beurre blanc before serving.

Serves 4
Cooking time: 2 hours
plus cooling time
Equipment: Stand mixer

2 large sea bass, weighing approx. 600g each, filleted (ask your fishmonger)

1 fennel bulb, core removed and finely sliced

Vegetable oil, for frying

16 new potatoes

Salt crust

700g of sea salt

900g of plain flour

3 eggs, separated

10g of dried mixed herbs

Pancakes

2 eggs

260ml of whole milk

120g of plain flour

1 tbsp chopped chives

1 tbsp chopped parsley

Lettuce

40g of carrot, finely diced

35g of shallot, finely diced

2 little gem lettuce, halved and core removed

60ml of white wine

160ml of fish stock, or chicken stock

Ingredients continue overleaf

Begin by making the salt crust. Place all the ingredients (apart from the egg yolks) in the bowl of a stand mixer with a dough hook attached, then mix on a medium speed. Slowly add water until a dough forms, then flatten the dough into a disc. Wrap in cling film and rest in the fridge for 30 minutes.

To make the pancakes, whisk together all the ingredients (apart from the oil) with a pinch of salt. Add a dash of oil to a wide frying pan and add an eighth of the batter to create a thin pancake, then set to one side and repeat 7 more times to create 8 pancakes. Note that these aren't eaten – they're used as a barrier between the salt crust and the fish, so don't worry if they don't look presentable.

Gently cook the sliced fennel in a frying pan with a dash of oil and a pinch of salt until soft with a slight crunch but without colour (around 6 minutes), then set aside to cool.

To cook the lettuce, add a dash of oil to a pan and gently cook the carrot and shallot for 5 minutes. Nestle the halved lettuces flat-side down on top, then pour in the wine and bring to the boil. Pour in the stock, add a pinch of salt and pepper then cover the lettuces with a sheet of baking paper. Reduce the heat and leave to cook for 10 minutes, until the lettuces are cooked through but not mushy. Set aside to reheat later.

Around 40 minutes before you plan to serve, preheat an oven to 200°C. Unwrap the rested salt dough and divide it in half. Roll both halves out on a floured work surface into roughly the same shape as the bass fillets, but larger. Lay one half of the salt dough onto a baking tray.

Recipe continues overleaf

Ingredients and recipe continued

Chive beurre blanc

60ml of white wine

10ml of white wine vinegar

40g of shallot, finely chopped

20ml of double cream

125g of unsalted butter, diced

1 bunch of chives, finely chopped

Arrange 2 of the pancakes next to each other on top of the salt dough so they slightly overlap. Remove the skin from 1 of the sea bass fillets, then place it on top of the pancakes and lightly season with salt. Spread half of the softened fennel on top of the fish, then top with a non-skinned fillet, skin-side up, and season lightly again. Place 2 more pancakes on top and tuck them in, so the fish is completely covered with the pancakes. Repeat this with the remaining 2 fillets and 4 pancakes, so you have 2 pancake-wrapped parcels of fish and fennel. Arrange these packages on the salt dough, trying to keep them apart so they don't stick together but with some dough still exposed around each edge.

Brush the exposed dough around the pancakes with the reserved egg yolks from making the crust, then carefully place the other half of the dough on top, pushing the edges down so it is completely sealed. Bake for 20 minutes.

Meanwhile, boil the potatoes in salted water for 15 minutes, or until tender and gently reheat the lettuces.

For the beurre blanc, add the wine, vinegar and shallot to a saucepan and simmer over a medium heat until almost completely dry and syrupy. Pour in the cream, return to the boil then gently stir in the butter. Pass through a fine sieve into a clean pan, then season and stir in the chives.

To serve, divide the potatoes and lettuces between serving plates. Use the beurre blanc to dress the potatoes, with any extra on the side. Bring the plates to the table along with the salt-baked fish, then use a serrated knife to carefully cut open the long side of the crust in front of your guests. Fold it back, then gently peel away the pancakes – take care as they can easily take the fish skin with them. Cut the fish into equal portions at the table.

Make-Ahead
Desserts

Butterscotch panna cotta with blackberries and gingernut crumb

Rich, wobbly, yielding panna cottas are flavoured with vanilla and caramel then served with juicy blackberries and a ginger and hazelnut crumb in this easy make-ahead recipe. Adding a pinch of salt to the cream results in a salted caramel-like flavour and you can replace the blackberries with whatever fruit is in season.

Serves 4
Cooking time: 45 minutes
plus 2 hours setting time
Equipment: 4x125ml moulds

Panna cottas

300ml of double cream

150ml of whole milk

¼ vanilla pod, split and seeds scraped, or ¼ tsp vanilla extract

1½ gelatine leaves

100g of caster sugar

Blackberries

100g of blackberries

2 tbsp caster sugar

1 squeeze of lemon juice

Crumb

20g of blanched hazelnuts, roughly chopped

3 ginger biscuits

1 lemon, zested

Pour the cream, milk and vanilla seeds into a saucepan and place the gelatine into a bowl of cold water to soften. Gently bring the cream mixture to the boil.

Meanwhile, pour the sugar into a separate pan and place over a medium heat. Cook, swirling rather than stirring, until the sugar melts and turns a light golden colour. Carefully pour the hot cream into the caramel, stirring constantly, until well combined. Squeeze the gelatine leaves to drain, then stir them into the warm cream until dissolved. Add a small pinch of salt, then pass the mixture through a fine sieve into 4 moulds, bowls or ramekins – you should have around 125ml per serving. Cover and place in the fridge to set for at least 2 hours.

Preheat an oven to 180°C. While you wait, halve the blackberries and place in a small pan with the sugar and a squeeze of lemon juice. Cook over a low heat for 5 minutes, or until the berries just start to soften and release their juice. Reserve in the fridge until needed.

Place the hazelnuts on a baking tray and into the oven for 7-10 minutes, stirring regularly, until golden all over. Transfer to a bowl, then crumble in the biscuits and stir in the lemon zest. Cover and set aside until needed.

To serve, boil a kettle and pour some hot water into a deep tray. Dip the base of the panna cotta moulds into the hot water for a few seconds, then turn them out onto plates. The bottoms of the panna cottas should have melted, creating a glossy sauce. Garnish with a pinch of crumble and some blackberries, with a drizzle of the blackberry juices to finish.

Toasted oat, rhubarb and cardamom frangipane tart

Frangipane tarts can form the base for all sorts of fruit and flavourings; here it provides a rich, sweet foil against the tartness of rhubarb and the fragrance of cardamom. The toasted oats in the pastry also add a surprising amount of flavour and provide a little crunch. Get creative with your rhubarb placement – we've kept it simple here, but if you have the time a little tessellation will guarantee wow-factor.

Serves 6-8
Cooking time: 2 hours
plus resting time
Equipment: 23cm fluted tart tin, food processor

Pastry

130g of oats

150g of plain flour, plus extra for dusting

60g of icing sugar

½ tsp salt

150g of unsalted butter, chilled and diced

1 egg

Filling

125g of unsalted butter, softened, plus extra for greasing

125g of golden caster sugar

1 egg

125g of ground almonds

20 cardamom pods, green husks lightly bashed and removed and the black seeds ground to a powder

200g of rhubarb, sliced into whatever shape you like

Crème fraîche, to serve

Preheat an oven to 180°C. Place the oats on a baking tray and bake for around 10 minutes, or until golden, stirring every few minutes to make sure they don't burn. Leave to cool, then blitz in a food processor to a fine powder. Add the flour, icing sugar, salt and butter then blitz again until it becomes sandy in consistency. Add the egg and pulse a few times until it comes together as a dough, then flatten into a disc, wrap in cling film and rest in the fridge for 1 hour.

Grease a 23cm tart tin with a removable base with butter, then dust with flour. Roll the dough out between 2 sheets of baking paper until around 5mm thick, then transfer to the tart case, leaving plenty of overhang. Prick the base with a fork all over, then return to the fridge for another 30 minutes. This is important, as it stops the pastry shrinking during cooking.

Preheat an oven to 170°C. Place a sheet of foil on top of the pastry, moulding it into the sides. Fill the foil with baking beans or dried rice, then place in the oven to blind-bake for 10 minutes. Remove the beans and foil and bake for another 5 minutes, then leave to cool slightly. Use a serrated knife to carefully trim away the overhang.

To make the filling, beat the butter and sugar together until light and creamy, then mix in the egg. Stir in the ground almonds and ground cardamom, then spoon this mixture into the pastry case. Top with the rhubarb, then bake for another 35-40 minutes, or until the frangipane is set and the tart is a deep golden all over – a little light charring around the edges is fine. Leave to cool for 10 minutes before removing from the tin, then leave to cool completely.

To serve, slice the tart and plate up with a generous dollop of crème fraîche.

Olive oil cake with thyme jelly and elderflower cream

Using olive oil instead of butter in a cake gives it a dense, moist texture, which means it'll keep for longer without going stale. Flavoured with lemon and served with a palate cleansing thyme jelly along with floral elderflower-infused cream, this is a perfect cake for when summer is just over the horizon.

Serves 6-8

Cooking time: 1 hour 15 minutes

plus 3-4 hours setting time and cooling time

Equipment: 23cm cake tin, electric whisk

Olive oil cake

2 large eggs

250g of golden caster sugar

100ml of extra virgin olive oil, plus extra for greasing

180g of whole milk

1 lemon

170g of plain flour, plus extra for dusting

1 tsp baking powder

¼ tsp bicarbonate of soda

Thyme jelly

2 gelatine leaves

1 lemon

20g of caster sugar

250ml of water

1 bunch of thyme, leaves picked

Elderflower cream

150g of double cream

40g of elderflower liqueur, or cordial

3 tsp icing sugar

Elderflowers, to garnish (optional)

Begin by making the jelly, as it needs 3-4 hours to set. Soak the gelatine leaves in a bowl of cold water for 5-10 minutes. Meanwhile, zest the lemon and set aside. Squeeze the juice into a small pan, then add the sugar and water. Taste and make sure you're happy with the flavour – add more sugar or lemon juice if needed. Bring to a simmer, then remove from the heat.

Squeeze the gelatine leaves to drain, then stir them into the pan until dissolved. Pour into a plastic container, stir in some thyme leaves, then place in the fridge to set for at least 3-4 hours. After 1 hour of setting time, give the mixture a stir to ensure the thyme is distributed evenly throughout.

Preheat an oven to 170°C and grease and flour a 23cm cake tin with a removable base. Use an electric whisk to beat the eggs and sugar together for 5 minutes until pale and doubled in volume, then stir in the olive oil, milk and reserved lemon zest. Zest and juice the other lemon, then add this in too. Sift the plain flour, baking powder, bicarbonate of soda and a pinch of salt into the mixture, then carefully fold together, trying not to knock the air out of the eggs as you work.

Pour the batter into the cake tin and bake for 40-50 minutes. It's ready when a skewer inserted into the centre comes out clean. If the top of the cake becomes too dark, cover with foil.

While the cake bakes, whip the double cream to soft peaks with an electric whisk, then stir in the elderflower liqueur (or cordial) and icing sugar. Reserve in the fridge.

Allow the cake to cool for a few minutes before removing from the tin, then place on a wire rack to cool completely. To serve, slice the cake and serve with a spoonful of jelly and a dollop of cream. Garnish with elderflowers if you have them.

Sesame and pink grapefruit treacle tart

Zingy pink grapefruit adds welcome freshness while toasted sesame seeds lend a nutty note to this incredible treacle tart. The miso paste takes on a similar role to the salt in salted caramel, accentuating the sweetness of the filling rather than changing the flavour overall. A spoonful of clotted cream dusted with tart sumac finishes things off wonderfully.

Serves: 6-8
Cooking time: 1 hour 15 minutes
plus resting and cooling time
Equipment: 23cm fluted tart tin, food processor

Pastry

280g of plain flour, plus extra for dusting

½ tsp fine salt

140g of unsalted butter, chilled and cubed, plus extra for greasing

1 medium egg

Filling

60g of sesame seeds

450g of golden syrup

1 pink grapefruit, zested and juiced

100g of fresh breadcrumbs

½ tsp white miso paste

1 piece of stem ginger in syrup, finely chopped

2 tbsp double cream

1 medium egg

To serve

150g of clotted cream

½ tsp sumac

Begin with the pastry. Place the flour, salt and butter in a food processor and blitz into a sandy texture, then add the egg and blend again until it comes together as a dough, adding a little cold water if needed. Tip out onto a work surface and bring together into a ball. Flatten the ball into a disc then wrap in cling film and rest in the fridge for 1 hour.

Grease and flour the tart tin. Roll the dough out between 2 sheets of baking paper until roughly 5mm thick, then transfer to the tin, leaving a few centimetres of overhang all the way around. Prick the base with a fork and place back in the fridge for 30 minutes – this is an important step as it stops the pastry shrinking while it bakes.

Preheat an oven to 170°C. Place a sheet of foil in the pastry-lined tart case and push it into the sides to ensure it is flush against the pastry right the way around. Fill with baking beans or dry rice and bake for 10 minutes. Remove the beans and foil and cook for another 5 minutes, then leave to cool slightly (leave the oven on). Use a serrated knife to carefully carve off any overhanging pastry, then set aside to cool completely.

To make the filling, place the sesame seeds on a tray and toast in the oven for 5 minutes or until golden. Be sure to stir halfway through as they can burn very quickly.

Place the golden syrup in a pan along with the grapefruit zest, 2 tablespoons of the grapefruit juice, the breadcrumbs, toasted sesame seeds, miso paste, stem ginger, double cream and egg. Gently heat, stirring to combine, then pour the mixture into the tart case. Bake for 30 minutes, then leave to cool completely.

To serve, slice the tart into 6-8 pieces, then plate up with a spoonful of clotted cream dusted with sumac.

Charred nectarine and mascarpone Pavlova

Few puddings turn a head like a Pavlova, piled high with whipped cream and juicy fruit. By both charring and poaching the nectarines, there's a nice contrast in texture. The basil leaves aren't just there to look pretty – they add a fragrant, fresh top note to the dish.

Serves 6-8
Cooking time: 1 hour 20 minutes
plus cooling time
Equipment: Electric whisk

Meringue

6 egg whites

375g of caster sugar

1 tsp balsamic vinegar

1 tbsp cornflour

Nectarines

250ml of Sauternes, or another dessert wine

150ml of water

1 strip of lemon peel

25g of caster sugar

4 ripe nectarines

½ tsp icing sugar

Mascarpone cream

200g of mascarpone

150ml of double cream

2 tbsp icing sugar

Basil leaves, to garnish

Preheat an oven to 120°C. Use an electric whisk to whip the egg whites into stiff peaks, then add the sugar a little at a time, whisking as you go, until thick and glossy. Fold in the vinegar and cornflour, then spoon the meringue onto a tray lined with baking paper. Use a spatula to shape it into a circle around 6cm high with a slight dip in the middle. Bake for 1 hour, then turn off the oven and leave the meringue inside to cool.

Meanwhile, place the wine, water, lemon peel and caster sugar into a saucepan large enough to hold 2 of the nectarines in a single layer. Bring to the boil, stirring until the sugar has dissolved, then reduce to a simmer.

Cut a small cross in the base of 2 of the nectarines, then poach in the liquid for 5-10 minutes, depending on ripeness, until the skin starts to peel away from the fruit. Lift them out of the syrup, leave to cool slightly, then carefully peel off the skins. Place the skins back in the liquid (this will give it a beautiful pink colour), then simmer the liquid for 5 minutes until syrupy. Strain through a fine sieve and leave to cool.

Cut the poached nectarines into wedges, discarding the stone, then reserve in the fridge. Place a griddle pan over a high heat and wait until it is smoking hot. Meanwhile, cut the remaining 2 nectarines into wedges, discarding the stone. Sprinkle the wedges with icing sugar, then cook the nectarines on each side for 3 minutes, until charred and soft in the centre. Reserve in the fridge until needed.

Whip the mascarpone, cream and icing sugar together using an electric whisk until they form soft peaks, then cover and reserve in the fridge.

When ready to serve, transfer the meringue to a serving plate and dollop the mascarpone cream all over. Arrange slices of the poached and charred nectarines on top, then drizzle with the syrup. Finish with basil leaves and bring to the table.

Chocolate orange fondants with Cointreau cream

Chocolate and orange – what's not to like? A dessert that will never fall out of fashion, these puds only require a quick blast in the oven before serving. Both the fondants and cream can be prepared a day in advance. If you don't have darioles, then you can simply bake the mixture in heatproof serving bowls.

Serves 6
Cooking time: 45 minutes
Equipment: 6x150ml darioles,
electric whisk

200g of dark chocolate

50g of unsalted butter, plus extra for greasing

2 oranges, zested, plus 2 tbsp juice

4 eggs

60g of light brown sugar

30g of plain flour

2 tsp cocoa powder, plus extra for dusting

100g double cream

3 tsp Cointreau

Grease 6 darioles then dust them in cocoa powder, tapping away any excess, then reserve in the fridge to set.

Place the dark chocolate and butter in a heatproof bowl set over a pan of simmering water to melt. You can also do this in the microwave in short bursts. Stir in the orange juice and three-quarters of the zest until fully combined, reserving the rest of the zest for garnishing.

Use an electric whisk to whisk the eggs and sugar together for 5 minutes until pale and doubled in size, then fold the melted chocolate and butter into them, followed by the flour and a pinch of salt.

Divide the fondant mixture between the darioles, then place in the fridge until ready to cook.

Pour the cream and Cointreau into a bowl and use an electric whisk to whip them together until they form stiff peaks. Reserve in the fridge until needed. If made far in advance, you may need to re-whip the cream if it has separated a little.

When ready to serve, preheat an oven to 180°C. Place the ramekins in the oven and bake for 12 minutes. Carefully tip out into serving dishes, then serve with the cream, reserved orange zest and a dusting of cocoa powder.

Hazelnut dacquoise with chocolate and coffee cream

A chance to show off your patisserie prowess at home, this magnificent dacquoise is comprised of layers of chewy hazelnut meringue, silky coffee-flavoured cream and rich dark chocolate ganache. Get creative with the shapes if you like – we've created individual circular stacks, but the dish also looks seriously impressive brought to the table in a single large tower.

Serves: 6
Cooking time: 1 hour
plus cooling time
Equipment: Food processor, electric whisk, piping bags

Hazelnut dacquoise

3 large egg whites

150g of caster sugar

¼ teaspoon cream of tartar

125g of blanched hazelnuts

15g of cornflour

Cocoa powder, for dusting

Toasted hazelnuts, finely chopped, to garnish (optional)

Coffee cream

300g of double cream

1 tbsp instant coffee powder

1 tbsp icing sugar

Chocolate ganache

125g of dark chocolate

125g of double cream

Use an electric whisk to whisk the egg whites until frothy. Start adding the sugar, a little at a time, whilst whisking constantly. Keep adding the sugar until you have around 2 tablespoons left – the meringue should be thick and glossy. Whisk in a pinch of salt and the cream of tartar.

Place the blanched hazelnuts in a food processor and blitz to a coarse powder – it should look slightly coarser than ground almonds. Mix them with the cornflour and remaining sugar, then carefully fold this mixture into the meringue until well incorporated but not overmixed.

Preheat an oven to 160°C. Line 3 baking trays with baking paper, then add 6 equal dollops of meringue to each tray. Use the back of a spoon to gently spread each dollop into a circle. Bake for 30 minutes, or until lightly browned, crisp on top and starting to come away from the paper. Leave to cool.

Meanwhile, make the coffee cream by whipping the ingredients together into stiff peaks (add a splash of whole milk if you accidentally over-whisk and it begins to separate). Transfer to a piping bag and reserve in the fridge.

For the chocolate ganache, break the chocolate up into small pieces and place in a heatproof bowl. Bring the cream to a boil, then pour it over the chocolate. Stir together until combined, then leave to cool.

When ready to serve, it's time to assemble. Place a piece of meringue on a serving platter. Use a spatula to spread some of the ganache on top, then pipe over a layer of cream. Repeat this process once again, then top the dacquoise with the final layer of meringue. Spread over a little more ganache and cream, then repeat to create 5 more stacks. Dust with cocoa powder and sprinkle with chopped hazelnuts (if using).

Peach Melba roulade
by Graham Hornigold

Peach, raspberry, vanilla, white chocolate and almond make up the star-studded cast of this deliciously retro roulade from acclaimed pastry chef Graham Hornigold. The four elements can all be made a day in advance if desired, leaving you to simply assemble and roll up on the day of serving.

Serves 8-10
Cooking time: 1 hour
plus overnight resting time
Equipment: Stand mixer, Swiss roll tray (approx. 35x30cm), stick blender

Sponge

6 eggs

150g of caster sugar

70g of T45 flour, or 00 flour, sifted

20g of flaked almonds

Ganache

8g of liquid glucose

110g of whipping cream

½ vanilla pod

15g of white chocolate, broken into small pieces

25g of marzipan, crumbled

Peaches

1 tbsp honey

2 peaches, halved and stone removed

Compote

250g of frozen raspberries

2 tbsp caster sugar

To serve

1 punnet of raspberries

Icing sugar, for dusting

Begin by making the ganache, as it needs to rest overnight. Pour the liquid glucose and 40g of the cream into a saucepan with the vanilla seeds (reserving the pod). Bring to the boil, then pour over the white chocolate and marzipan and whisk to combine. Add the remaining cream then use a stick blender to blitz until smooth. Cover and place in the fridge overnight.

To poach the peaches, add the honey to a saucepan over a high heat. Cook until it begins to caramelise and darken, then add the peaches, reserved vanilla pod and 250ml of water. Bring to a simmer and poach the peaches for 4-5 minutes, then drain, leave to cool, peel and dice. Reserve in the fridge.

Place the raspberries and sugar in a saucepan and simmer over a medium-low heat until most of the liquid has evaporated and you're left with a thick sauce. Reserve in the fridge.

For the sponge, preheat an oven to 170°C. Separate 3 of the eggs into yolks and whites. Add the egg yolks, whole eggs and 110g of the sugar to a stand mixer and whisk together for 7-8 minutes until thick and fluffy. Meanwhile, whisk the egg whites into soft peaks in a separate bowl. Slowly add the remaining 40g of sugar until a thick meringue forms, then gently fold this into the whisked egg mixture, followed by the sifted flour.

Pour the sponge batter into a Swiss roll tray lined with baking paper. Sprinkle with the flaked almonds, then bake for 10-12 minutes. Leave to cool completely, then cover with cling film.

When ready to serve, whisk the chilled ganache into soft peaks. Turn out the sponge onto a tea towel and peel off the baking paper. Spread the sponge with a layer of raspberry compote, followed by the ganache, poached peaches and most of the fresh raspberries, then use the tea towel to help you roll it up along the longest side. Transfer to a serving dish, seam-side down, then dust with icing sugar and garnish with the remaining raspberries.

Summer pudding
by Roberta Hall-McCarron

A mighty, magnificent pud that's a joy to assemble and can be easily adapted to whatever berries you have to hand, Roberta's dessert is given extra summertime oomph thanks to the fragrant flavours of lemon thyme and elderflower.

Serves 6
Cooking time: 45 minutes
plus 4-5 hours setting time
Equipment: 18x7cm bowl, electric whisk

300ml of elderflower cordial

300g of frozen mixed fruits or berries

75g of cherries

100g of strawberries

100g of blueberries

100g of raspberries

50g of icing sugar

500g of sourdough, or more if it has a very thick crust

200ml of double cream

5g of lemon thyme, leaves picked and chopped

30g of white chocolate

Place the elderflower cordial and frozen mixed fruit in a saucepan over a medium heat and wait for the fruit to thaw. Meanwhile, de-stone the cherries and halve the strawberries (or quarter them if they are large). Once the frozen fruit has thawed, add the cherries, strawberries, blueberries and raspberries. Cook, stirring regularly and adding the icing sugar a little at a time, until the fruit begins to break down but is still holding its shape.

Place a sieve over a large bowl and tip the fruit in. Leave to strain for 10-15 minutes to get as much liquid out of the fruit as possible. Meanwhile, slice the sourdough into 1cm-thick slices and cut off the crusts. Soak the slices in the strained fruit juices (it's best to do this while the juices are still warm).

Line a bowl that's approximately 18cm in diameter and 7cm in height with cling film with plenty of excess overhang. Layer the soaked sourdough around the bowl, ensuring it is completely covered, reserving some slices for the top.

Use an electric whisk to whip the cream to soft peaks, then fold through 120g of the strained fruit and the lemon thyme. Place 3 tablespoons of the remaining fruit into the base of the sourdough-lined bowl, followed by a few tablespoons of the remaining juices. Spoon the whipped cream on top, flattening it with a spoon and ensuring there is 1cm of space at the top of the bowl. Cover with some more soaked sourdough slices, then bring the overhanging cling film up over the top to seal the pudding. Transfer to the fridge for at least 4-5 hours to firm up and set. Reserve any leftover fruit in the fridge too.

When ready to serve, carefully peel back the cling film and turn the pudding out onto a serving plate, gently pulling on the cling film to tease it out of the bowl. Remove the rest of the cling film, then garnish with the remaining fruit. Finish by grating over the white chocolate.

Dark chocolate 'pot du crème' with white chocolate truffle
by Stuart Collins

Simple yet devastatingly effective, Stuart Collins' double chocolate dessert combines a rich, firm dark chocolate custard with a scoop of fresher, lighter white chocolate on top, along with a scattering of cocoa nibs for crunch. Prepare both elements the day before and you'll be able to serve up in seconds.

Serves 6
Cooking time: 30 minutes
plus 4 hours setting time
Equipment: Thermometer, stick blender

Pot du crème

250g of dark chocolate, broken into small pieces

285g of whole milk

285g of double cream

110g of egg yolk (from approx. 6 eggs)

20g of caster sugar

15g of cocoa nibs

White chocolate truffle

100g of white chocolate, broken into small pieces

100g of crème fraîche

100g of double cream

For the pot du crème, place the dark chocolate in a heatproof bowl. Pour the milk and double cream into a pan and bring to a simmer. Meanwhile, whisk together the egg yolks, sugar and a small pinch of salt until thick and pale. Once the milk has come to a simmer, pour a splash of it into the eggs, whisking constantly, to temper, then slowly pour this mixture back into the hot cream.

Over a medium-low heat, gradually bring the mixture to 85°C, whilst whisking constantly, then pour this over the dark chocolate. Use a stick blender to emulsify and fully combine the mixture, then divide between 6 serving bowls and cover in cling film. Place in the fridge for at least 4 hours to set.

Place a heatproof bowl over a small pan of barely simmering water, ensuring the water isn't touching the base of the bowl. Add the white chocolate. Leave to melt, stirring occasionally, until the chocolate reaches a temperature of 36°C.

Meanwhile, whisk together the crème fraîche and cream until firm. As soon as the chocolate has melted and reached the required temperature, whisk it into the cream, then pour into a container, cover and reserve in the fridge until needed.

When ready to serve, ensure the bowls of dark chocolate custard have been out of the fridge for 30 minutes to allow them to come to room temperature. Dip a spoon in warm water and use it to scoop neat quenelles of the white chocolate truffle, placing them on top, then sprinkle over some cocoa nibs.